DIVINE
DILEMMA

WRESTLING
WITH THE QUESTION
OF A LOVING GOD
IN A FALLEN
WORLD

KEN HAM

First printing: June 2023
Second printing: July 2023

Master Books, P.O. Box 726, Green Forest, AR 72638

Master Books® is a division of the New Leaf Publishing Group, LLC.

ISBN: 978-1-68344-355-1
ISBN: 978-1-61458-866-5 (digital)
Library of Congress Control Number: 2023938152

Previously published as *How Could a Loving God?*

Cover by Left Coast Design

Printed in the United States of America

Please visit our website for other great titles:
www.masterbooks.com

For information regarding promotional opportunities, please contact the publicity department at pr@nlpg.com.

Introduction

My younger brother, a wonderful Christian preacher, died from an awful degenerative brain disease on June 9, 2002. As a result of this, in 2006 I wrote a book about the experience to help Christians answer the question of why God allows "good" people to suffer. I wrote this from the heart, applying a biblical worldview to give answers, and focused a lot on my dear godly mother and how we handled this sad situation.

The book was called *How Could a Loving God?* Well, now it's 2023 and I'm totally updating this book with a major rewrite that includes a lot more information. I have learned a lot about dealing with this topic over the years

My brother Robert.

Mum & Dad and all six children.
Robert is second from the left at the back.

from studying God's Word and having spoken to so many people about the topic of suffering as I've heard their stories of tragedies, horrible diseases, and so many other heartbreaking situations.

Can we truly understand why God allows such suffering even for people who love Him and have received His gift of salvation? The answer is yes!

In this book, I relate a true account of life, suffering, and death. I open myself up, sharing my own struggles and the emotional trauma of dealing with this issue. You will feel the struggle and perhaps identify with it. But there really are answers that give that peace we need:

> *And the peace of God, which surpasses all understanding, will guard your hearts and your minds in Christ Jesus* (Philippians 4:7).

Why?

$\mathcal{O}ne$ of the most asked questions I've received as a Christian proclaiming the truth of God's Word beginning in Genesis goes something like this, "How do we understand all the death, disease, and suffering in this world if there really is a loving God?"

Many have attempted to deal with this topic down through the years. But we must admit, this is one of the most difficult issues from a human perspective to understand and deal with. Do we have satisfactory answers?

We've heard of non-Christians who lived long lives, with seeming health and a peaceful death. Yet we've seen wonderful Christian men and women suffer greatly and die in pain. We agonize over why God would take a young Christian mother or father home, leaving a young family distraught trying to cope with such tragedy.

Don't we all as Christians identify with Jeremiah's words? *Why does the way of the wicked prosper? Why do all who are treacherous thrive?* (Jeremiah 12:1)

But it doesn't seem fair, Lord! We need more great Christian men and women who stand on Your Word, and yet so many talented, God-fearing people seem to die young, or by some painful disease, or end up suffering horrible tragedies in their lives. It just doesn't seem fair. My younger brother was a wonderful Christian man. He loved God's Word and loved to teach it. He believed God's Word beginning in Genesis. So many church leaders today compromise God's Word in Genesis, and some are now going soft on the LGBTQ worldview. It doesn't make sense that my brother died at a young age. Don't we need more, not less, men like this?

And Lord, Bethley, the beautiful Christian friend of my wife and I who was so gentle and kind, so loving, and yet suffered from cancer, dying an agonizing death at a young age, leaving a young family. It doesn't seem to make sense. And why did my good friend and colleague Dr. Tommy Mitchell die at a relatively young age? He was a great creationist speaker, and we need more of them, not less. Why did my close friend (he is like a brother) Buddy Davis, have a stroke that took away from him the phenomenal talent of music and speaking You had entrusted to him, and he had used to proclaim Your Word around the world? He could have ministered to so many more people. And my good friend John from Alabama — one minor accident and his life changed to a daily physical struggle. What about the five Christian college students on the way home from Bible college killed

BREAKING NEWS

Students killed in wrong-way crash

LIVE

Current, former Arkansas high school students identified as 5 killed in Wyoming wrong-way crash

Students from Arkansas were visiting Jackson Hole Bible college in Wyoming by a drunk driver? And there are so many more examples.

I'm sure we could come up with almost endless stories like this. Stories of tragedy and seemingly unfair and devastating situations of grief and suffering.

And, of course, I've had many atheists mock me on social media for believing in a God of love when they see death, disease, and suffering permeating this world. "Isn't your God powerful enough to overcome all this?" they say. And then, when discussing the abortion topic, we hear them say things like, "If abortion is wrong, why does your God allow millions of babies to die from miscarriages?" And I've also had people say to me, "If babies go to heaven when they die, and if you believe human life begins at fertilization, you should support abortion as all these children will go to heaven and not have to be born and maybe go to hell."

Atheists also claim the biblical God is genocidal as He killed so many people including men, women, and children at the time of the Flood. They also point to instances in the Bible when God told the Israelites to kill every man, woman, and child in a particular city such as recorded in 1 Samuel 15:3 where God told them to totally wipe out the Amalekites:

> *"Now go and strike Amalek and devote to destruction all that they have. Do not spare them, but kill both man and woman, child and infant, ox and sheep, camel and donkey."*

How do we answer all these agonized questions and hostile accusations?

I sometimes think about John the Baptist. He was the man prophesied about in Isaiah 40 and Malachi 3 and 4. He was called by God to prepare the way for the Lord Jesus Christ's ministry on earth. He baptized Christ. But then he was jailed and beheaded in prison. Does that seem fair to us as humans?

What about the time Herod commanded that all the boys aged two and under in Bethlehem be killed (Matthew 2), but an angel warned Joseph in a dream to take Mary and Jesus and flee to Egypt to protect them from this order? Why didn't God warn the other families of young boys? Or what about when Pharaoh ordered all of the Israelite boys to be killed at the time of Moses' birth as recorded in Exodus 1? Why did God allow all those children to die? Can we even imagine the grief this caused for these families? How can we possibly understand all this?

What about King David? God had Samuel anoint him to be king, but then King Saul set out to kill him, resulting in David having to flee and fight for his life. In Psalm 13, David seems to have sunk to an all-time low, feeling God had left him. David cries out: *How long, O LORD? Will you forget me forever? How long will you hide your face from me? How long must I take counsel in my soul and have sorrow in my heart all the day? How long shall my enemy be exalted over me?* (Psalm 13:1–2). Later on, David commits adultery with Bathsheba, and then, to try to cover it up, had her husband killed. He repents and God forgives him (though there are consequences). But God calls David *a man after my heart* (Acts 13:22). Does this sound right and just to fallible humans like us?

I think about Jeremiah and the battles he fought. God called him to be a prophet, but he was persecuted. I can understand him crying out *Why does the way of the wicked prosper? Why do all who are treacherous thrive?* (Jeremiah 12:1).

And then we all know about Job. God let the devil commit all sorts of terrible acts against him. He lost his family, his flocks, his health — in fact, he lost everything. Although God reveals some of what happened behind the scenes, Job didn't know what was happening. His friends counseled Job that it must be the result of some wrong he had done that he needed to repent of. But even with all this, how could Job say, *"Though he slay me, I will hope in him"* (Job 13:15). Would we be able to truly say that if God allowed the same to happen to us?

All this is seemingly nigh on impossible to try to even begin to understand from a Christian perspective, let alone from a non-Christian one.

The questions seem limitless. Why does God allow a dictator to rule North Korea and persecute and torture Christians? Why did God allow Nero to viciously kill so many Christians? Why does God allow dictators like those in Cuba or China to rail against God's people and cause such misery? Why would God allow a tragedy like 9/11 to occur in the USA? Why all the wars and the resulting suffering? Why was Hitler allowed to murder millions of Jews and others? Why does God allow little children to be sexualized by drag queens and predators? Why does God allow children and others to be trafficked? Why? Why? Why?

I've read many articles where people testify to being brought up in church, but they rejected Christianity because of their belief that there can't be a loving God with all the death, suffering, and disease that permeates this world. And then there are those who claim they were once Christians, but because of a tragedy or abuse or some other grievous circumstance they walked away from the Christian faith.

QUESTIONS:

Is he not all-powerful?

Is he unjust?

How can there be a God of love?

Even as Christians, we live with many of these questions. And let's be honest, we all struggle to make sense of all of this. Many times, we sort of just ignore or push away such questions, until something happens that brings it all to the forefront.

Tragedy Strikes

We buried what was left of Robert's body on the 12th of June, 2002, in a quiet cemetery on the outskirts of Brisbane, Australia.

Later in the day, we would gather with others in a public celebration of his life, but only those who were closest to him during his earthly life gathered around the freshly dug grave that morning. As the cool winter breeze blew through the forest and the Australian gum trees around us, we held each other close and sought comfort and rest in the words of the pastor and the words of Scripture. It was the end of a long road. For months, a disease called "frontal lobe dementia" had been slowly and persistently eroding the networks of cells in his brain. For months we stood by helplessly as the disease ate away at his independence and physical presence, contorting his

mind and body into a twisted, empty shell. Now, we were standing together, returning to the ground the body of our brother and friend. One who was also a husband and father.

There was a certain sense of relief and peace among us — and a thankfulness that his agonizing battle was now complete — but deep in our souls' stirred thoughts and feelings that would not rest, echoes of questions that could not be quieted.

Why Robert? He was a good man and devoted father and husband, serving as a pastor in a Bible-teaching, Bible-defending church? Why this way? The disease had robbed him of everything that he valued most … his mind, his ability to communicate the gospel, his awareness of those he loved and who loved him. Why now? Robert was only 43. His ministry, born out of sacrifice and determination, was beginning to grow. And his family would never again hear the counsel and comfort of their earthly father's voice, nor would they feel the guidance and touch of his

Robert as a young boy.   Robert as a young man.

caring hand. Why did this happen when they all needed him the most?

We stood at the grave for some time, quietly, with little left to say ... but the questions would not be silenced among us: Why? Why? Why?

As we wiped the dirt from our hands and said our last goodbyes, the questions hung heavy in the air. Underneath these questions was a deeper question still — a question that has perplexed mankind for ages, but was now amplified by our circumstances and our pain — and it was a question that demanded an answer: Why would a loving God allow, or even cause, such pain, decay, and death?

As the oldest sibling in the family, I felt the full weight of the question. How would I answer? I'm a Christian and

Robert with me when he had become a preacher.

I believe and love God's Word. I teach it all over the world. I preach the message of salvation and tell people about the wonderful God of love who created us; but how could I reconcile all of that with what had happened to my brother Rob? What was I to say to my mother, my own wife and children, my brothers and sisters, nieces, nephews, and so on?

And what about the non-Christians who looked on and saw our Christian family struggling to cope with this terrible disaster? What were they thinking; what were they asking? What could we tell them in the midst of this tragedy that would cause them to look to the God of the Bible?

As these thoughts swirled without rest, yet another question came up in my mind: What would Robert say about it all? As a devout and gifted teacher of the Word, what would be his answer to these questions? What would he have said about the Bible and the God it portrays, had he been able to understand what had happened to him? Would he be angry? Would he turn his back on the Word of God he so faithfully preached? What would he say to God if he had been able to comprehend the nature of his disease, decline, and death?

Robert's disease and illness, as you might imagine, had been a struggle for me and our whole family. No, there are no easy answers in one sense, but in my search for how I should respond as a Christian, I believe that light can be shed on this seemingly unfair, contradictory, and irreconcilable situation. After all, if the God of the Bible Rob believed in is real, and if His nature is as revealed in the pages of Scripture, then there has to be a way of reconciling what seems to be so grossly unjust with a just and holy Creator — otherwise nothing makes sense.

For decades I've known and taught that the Word of God makes sense out of confusion when it comes to issues of history, geography, family, anthropology, morality, paleontology, etc. Since my brother's death, and the deep soul-searching it has caused, I now also know that the truth of the Word can make sense out of the deepest confusion of the heart, offering answers to the most perplexing, painful issues a person can face.

As we now turn to the infallible Word of God, may we, by His mercy and grace, be given the ability to understand the past, live powerfully in the present, and look to the future with hope, knowing that God Himself has given us answers (though not every answer) to the questions we so desperately ask.

3

And It Was Good

To understand any event or circumstance one needs to start at the beginning.

> *In the beginning God created the heavens and the earth.... And God saw everything that he had made, and behold, it was very good* (Genesis 1:1, 31)

The words of Genesis chapters 1 and 2 present to us the incredible chronicle of the first six days of existence. From nothing, God created the heavens and an earth. He spoke forth the first rays of light, separating them from the darkness, then He made distinction between the heavens and the waters below. Gathering the waters into seas and forming the dry land, God then spoke into reality plants and trees of every kind. With His voice He scattered the stars and hung the sun and moon. Filling the waters with living creatures and the skies with flying creatures, He then filled the land with living creatures ... and then He declared that it was *good*.

But God was far from done. On day 6, God created the first two people, from whom all humanity would come. From the dust of the ground God shaped the first man, breathing life into his nostrils, and giving him dominion over everything else that had been created. God showed Adam that he was alone, as only he was made in God's image. God then formed a mate from the man's side, and together they began their rule over all that had been made ... and then God declared everything He had made was *very good*.

I believe that we are incapable of imagining the per-fection that existed in Eden at that time. The harmony, the beauty, the unity, the way everything worked together in peace … it was very good, but a glance at the morning newspaper or listening to the evening news makes it graphically evident that we no longer live in the beautiful world He originally made. Murder, divorce, abor-tion, starvation, sexual perversion of many kinds, and war are the norm now; devastation is common, punctuated by disasters that appear to be both natural and man-made. To get away from it all, many retreat toward undisturbed nature, but even there — no, particularly there — we find the world can be extremely disturbing.

Whenever I mention my homeland of Australia, people often say, "Australia is such a wonderful country." It is. It's a tremendous country. It's a wonderful country … compared to many others. But let's be honest; it can also be a rough place. We have some of the most dangerous sea creatures on the planet. Some of our sea stingers will happily kill you in minutes, and our sharks will eat you so fast that no one will know what happened to you. The bite of many of our spiders can be the beginning of a slow and excruciating death. We have some of the most dangerous snakes in the world, too. Australia is also home to the most dangerous octopus in the

Yes, Australia has a phenomenal beauty.

world. If you are walking along a rocky shoreline and accidentally step on the octopus, you'll be dead within the hour. We have the most dangerous croc-

But you never know what is lurking around.

odiles in the world. We even have a deadly stinging tree! If you were to just brush up against the leaves of this tree, you would receive a painful sting that can last for years.

So, imagine you've come to Australia for a vacation to get away from "the real world" for a while. While walking on one of our "wonderful" nature trails, let's just say you brush up against the stinging tree. The pain is so great that you rush down the hillside to the nearby ocean to wash your arm. Immediately you get stung by one of the deadly tropical sea stingers, which almost immediately makes you dizzy and delirious (not to mention the pain), so you crawl out of the ocean and fall into a nearby freshwater creek, and "chomp!" just like that you become lunch for one of our man-eating crocodiles. Isn't Australia a beautiful country?

I think we are sometimes very guilty of giving the wrong idea to the non-Christian when we look at nature and say, "Look how beautiful this world is! Can't you see there's a God?" And they're looking at this world and you know what they see? People dying, tragedies, suffering, death, disease — they don't see a beautiful world.

I even think we sometimes give the wrong message to our kids through many of our Sunday school programs. When we want to talk to kids about God being "the great Designer" or "the great Creator," we often turn to nature as an example of His creative "beauty." Look at the pictures you see in the Sunday school books and in Christian school textbooks, aren't they "beautiful"? Sure, look how God beautifully designed this fox to rip the insides out of the bunny! See the dinosaur bones? Yeah, his body was crushed under the weight of tons of sediment. Look how that mosquito sucks the blood out of that little fawn! We point at nature and life and teach our kids to sing "All things bright and beautiful! The Lord God made them all!" Maybe we should be teaching them to sing "All things maimed and mangled! The Lord God judged them all!"

A friend of mine lived in the mountains near the coast

south of Brisbane. He said, "I take my non-Christian friends up on the mountain here, and we look over this beautiful countryside and the beach and I say, 'Can't you see there's a God? Look at the beautiful world He made!'" I differ with him. What we see in Australia is not the world that God made — and it's only beautiful compared to certain other places! At those beaches around Brisbane, you're liable to have the blue ringed octopus and sea stingers bring an abrupt end to your beautiful afternoon outing.

No, it's not a totally beautiful world; it's quite a dangerous and deadly one. Now there certainly is beauty in this world, but it's a world of beauty and ugliness, a world of life and death. It all seems so contradictory. In nature, we do see a remnant of beauty, a shattered reflection of the original perfection of Eden. But it's all in the context of death and destruction … all of it. Take the Grand Canyon, for example. If you took a non-Christian to this magnificent place — and it is magnificent, by the way; the views are indescribable, particularly at sunrise and sunset — and the two of you were sitting on the edge of the mile-deep canyon, and you say to your friend, "Can't you see there is a God of love in the beauty of what He has created?" Would

that be an accurate lead-in to a spiritual conversation? Is nature really an illustration of His love?

Certainly, there is a beauty there, but it's actually a result of judgment. The Grand Canyon wasn't a part of the original creation, it was formed from a cataclysmic act of God's judgment on a wicked world, a violent global flood that tore into the earth and entombed billions of living organisms.

That's the real bigger picture, and to communicate something else to a non-believer isn't communicating the fullness of biblical Christianity.

I remember being in the British Museum in London. It's an impressive place, filled with a massive collection of statues and artifacts that the British have obtained from around the

world over the years. I was watching a group looking at one of the statues from ancient Greece. It was missing part of the head, both arms, and part of the torso. Still, it stood tall, the white marble shining in the light. People were looking at it, saying, "Wonderful!" "Inspiring!" "Beautiful!" But a little boy nearby said, "What are you talking about? It looks all broken to me!"

Both observations were correct, of course. The adults could imagine the beauty in the fact that a tremendously talented sculptor had, at one time, captured the wonder of the human physique in stone … but the boy saw it for what it was today: a very broken and damaged sculpture. And you know, it is really the same with this earth. How many times do we as people look at this earth and say, "Look at this beautiful world and the trees and the birds and look at the other animals. Isn't this a beautiful world that God made?" Well, I've got news for you: it all looks broken to me. It's a broken and damaged world. And when we use nature as an example of God's beauty and love, we can be giving the wrong idea if we're not explaining it correctly.

The animated movie *Madagascar* does a great job of playing off of this. (That's a great movie, by the way; very funny.) At one point all these animals are skipping through the forest. They've recently escaped from the zoo to find a better life in the wild. As they meander through the woods, the song "What a Wonderful World," first sung by Louie Armstrong, is playing in the background … but every time they turn around, an animal jumps out of the bushes and grabs some cute little furry creature and rips its head off, or swallows it, or puts the squeeze on it.

The irony is hysterical. Sure, it's very funny in an animated movie like *Madagascar*, but it's not so funny when it's in your own neighborhood, or in your own family. This world is filled with disease, destruction, decay, and death … and when it comes to our home, the ramifications can spread like shock waves through every aspect of our being.

Facing Reality

On the telephone in Australia, 10,000 miles away, my sister was trying to describe my brother's physical appearance. "Do you remember the TV programs that showed those horrible pictures of prisoners from the concentration camps?" she asked. "Remember how thin they looked from starvation? Kenny, in a way, Robert reminds me of them." I tried to imagine it; then, as the image appeared in my mind, I tried to not imagine it. All I knew was that I wanted to see my younger brother at least one more time. He was so young — early forties — how could this be happening to him? I boarded a plane for 20 hours of flying, giving me lots of time to reflect on the past and contemplate the future.

A few hours after arriving in Australia, I walked into the nursing home with my mother. My visit was a surprise for her, but our joyful reunion quickly dissolved into tears as my mother conveyed what had taken place the last several weeks. I hadn't seen Robert for a few months, and I knew that no matter how hard I tried, I would not be prepared for what I was about to experience.

My heart began to race as we walked the corridors of the nursing home. It was a pathetic sight. In one large area, a dozen or so mostly elderly people sat in silence, gazing into nowhere. One lady whistled continually while another kept saying certain words over and over again. Periodic groans were heard from a man in the corner, and beside him another lady kept moving her legs and body in a peculiar continual motion. Some sat motionless, their contorted faces and glassy eyes glued on the television. Only one person seemed aware of my presence, but when he spoke, the words were fragmented and unintelligible.

Inside, my heart was breaking. I was looking at someone's wife and mother, a husband and father, a son or daughter. On the walls hung pictures of some of these people — images of life before the horrible sicknesses overtook them. The contrast was so stark it was hard to believe I was looking at the same people.

This was a Christian nursing home. Most of these patients were dedicated believers — Sunday school teachers, deacons, and devoted parents. One 78-year-old man in a room nearby had been an active evangelist. His family was gathered around him as he was breathing his last after a seven-year battle with Alzheimer's disease.

Then I saw Robert. He was lying there, hardly moving. He showed very little (if any) signs of recognition of his mother and eldest brother. Mum tenderly stroked his forehead and then began the arduous task of trying to get him to swallow a special drink she had prepared for him. Increasingly, his swallowing ability was disappearing. His food had to be put through a blender and fed to him teaspoon by teaspoon or through a drinking cup. He would swallow and then choke; swallow and then choke. Mum would wipe his face and wait to give him another sip. At times, tears would run down her face. She was so patient and so loving, talking to him and caring for him just as one would for a baby. At times, we both held his hands. He would look at us, and once or twice I wondered whether I saw a flash of recognition in his facial expressions — and then it was gone.

Mum and Dad in early 60s — Robert is front left.

Mum and Dad and family after number 6 came — Robert on far right.

Divine Dilemma

My mother in her later years.

Yes, when disease, destruction, decay, or death come "home," it's time for a difficult reality check. In those hours we stare life — real life — in the eyes, and face issues that can often be avoided in the course of normal life. Perhaps you've been there too. Maybe you're there now, facing the bitter realities of life and death. Even if you haven't, make no mistake, you will face these realities soon enough — and with the reality comes questions.

Questions

The issues of suffering and death beg one of the most perplexing and pressing questions that's being asked in our culture: "How can there be a God of love with so much death and suffering in the world?" The question is far from hypothetical or philosophical; it's both theological and highly practical ... and it's usually asked when we face what appears to be a tragic inconsistency in the world.

Whenever there's been a major tragedy such as the one that resulted in many thousands killed in Turkey and Syria from a devastating earthquake in February 2023, people ask

Destruction from 2023 earthquake in Hatay, Turkey.
Photo by: Hilmi Hacaloğlu; Public Domain via Wikimedia Commons

questions such as where was God when that happened? And what about all the wars that saw so many killed and maimed and countless people suffering as a result? What about the Holocaust? I mean, how could there be a God of love?

The Christian believes that God is love that God cares, that He is present everywhere, and that He is all powerful. His Word clearly teaches this. We believe that He knows everything and is merciful and forgiving. We believe that God created the universe and everything in it, declaring that it was "very good." And yet even superficial observations indicate we've got some "problems." How do we reconcile what we see and what we believe as Christians?

We look at massive famine in Africa. We hear of girls suffering at the hands of their own fathers in our own neighborhoods. Just think about death in general (let alone the death of those who are young and "innocent"). It doesn't seem right at all, and people get angry at God over these things. "How can there be a God of love if he allows this?

How can you Christians believe in your God of love? Why would a God of love let my mother die, or my wife die? If you are a God of love, why would you do this?" How do we understand it? How do we put all that together?

I don't think I can overstate the importance of answering the questions correctly. All we have to do is look at how some non-Christians in the world have responded to this sort of thing. Consider, for example, CNN founder Ted Turner. A man of great wealth and a bitter heart, he is leaving a powerful legacy in the atheistic media. It's easy to view him as an enemy of sorts but let me give you something to think about. Consider this quote from an interview he had with *The New York Times*:

> Turner is a strident nonbeliever having lost his faith after his sister Mary Jane died of a painful disease. "I was taught that God was love and God was powerful," Turner said, "I couldn't understand how someone so innocent should be made or allowed to suffer so."[1]

Turner is not an isolated case. Some of the most atheistic, humanistic, ardent opponents of our creation ministry claim they were brought up in Bible-believing churches — and yet heart-wrenching circumstances caused them to walk away from their faith. You know what I believe has happened? Many were brought up in churches where Christianity was imposed upon them, but they weren't taught how to defend the Christian faith. They never learned to interpret circumstances with

---

1. Ted Turner, "Ted Turner Was Suicidal After Breakup," NYTimes. com, April 16, 2001.

the truth of the Word. Instead, they grew up interpreting the
Bible according to their circumstances. This is why the way
you communicate truth to people is really important.

Some people believe that, when sharing with an unbeliever, you should never start from God's Word but use evidence to try to convince them God is real. But all evidence
is interpreted depending on the worldview you have, which
is based on the foundation of God's Word or man's word.
Think about it — if we start from the circumstances of this
world, we see death, suffering, and disease. Thus, if there is
a God, He must be an ogre. It's only when you start from
God's Word, beginning in Genesis 1–11, that we can begin
to look at this evidence correctly.

In many cases, I believe these people mentioned above
were in churches that didn't take Genesis 1–11 as literal history but compromised with evolution and millions of years.
Thus, for them, death and suffering were a part of how God
created everything and have existed for millions of years.
They were not taught death and disease are the result of our
sin. When they faced the tension of difficult questions about
evil and suffering, the circumstances and lack of teaching
concerning the true origin of death led them to believe that
God either didn't exist or that He was uncaring or passive.

Significantly, we see this again in the life of Charles
Darwin. Darwin grew up going to church (one that was
not founded on the Bible being inerrant like Bible-believing
churches today) and his family continued to do so after he
married. But Darwin had a daughter named Annie, and
when she became ill, Charles' life was deeply impacted. It is
said in his biography that:

Any vestige of belief in God left him when his daughter Annie died. Annie's cruel death destroyed Charles' tatters and belief in a moral and just universe. Later he would say that this period claimed the final death nail for his Christianity. Charles now took his stand as an unbeliever.[2]

In 2001, PBS broadcast a series on evolution. In the episode called "Darwin's Dangerous idea," they covered the life of Darwin. At one point in the documentary, Darwin's family enters a church but Darwin himself remains outside, lingering by Annie's grave. Then we hear the people in the church singing the hymn, "All things bright and beautiful, the Lord God made them all." Obviously, the producers of this documentary series wanted people to see that Christianity supposedly teaches that God made everything beautiful, but Darwin is outside in an ugly graveyard of death thinking about the death of his daughter. How could there be a loving God? It's the same irony we found in the movie *Madagascar*, except in Darwin's case, the loss of his daughter was real, the tears he shed were real ... and the questions he wrestled with deep in his soul were real. Finding no suitable answers to the issues that tormented his soul, he turned his back totally on Christianity, and set out to explain the origin of life without God.

And that's something we also need to understand. Darwinian evolution was really formulated to try to explain life by natural processes — without God. It's the religion of atheism. It's so sad that so many church leaders have com-

2. A. Desmond and J. Moore, *Darwin: The Life of a Tormented Evolutionist* (New York: W.W. Norton & Company, 1991), p. 387.

THE LIFE OF
A TORMENTED
EVOLUTIONIST

"Unquestionably, the finest [biography] ever
written about Darwin. . . . Darwin has now
become, and properly, the quintessentially
socially embedded scientist. Desmond and
Moore are brilliant in their relentless and
integrative pursuit of this truly unifying
theme."
———————— *STEPHEN JAY GOULD*

ADRIAN DESMOND
& JAMES MOORE

promised Darwin's ideas with Genesis. It's a major reason why these leaders can't teach the correct answers to people concerning issues like death and suffering. That's why so many in our churches don't know how to deal with this issue.

It's easy to point the finger at non-Christians who have struggled with "the question." But the Christian response in many instances hasn't been much better. Many tend to ignore the issue altogether; some just hide the doubt under the surface of their faith while others cloak the problem under a cover-

Charles Darwin statue in the Natural History Museum, London.
Credit: Maria Suter

ing of spiritual sounding clichés. So many have not been taught from God's Word as they should have to know how to deal with this.

I think one of the reasons that many people — and many young people — in our churches struggle with their faith is because the teaching and music give the message that the Christian life is supposed to be carefree and problem free. We teach children songs that say "I'm happy all the time. Since Jesus Christ came in, and saved my soul from sin … I'm happy all the time."

Meanwhile, they are getting beat up on the playground, watching the latest headline news, and listening to their parents fight in the evening. Nowhere does Scripture promise a totally "happy" life, and we should not insinuate otherwise. Again, we point at nature and try to tell them it's all good and beautiful, but in reality, it is literally a "dog-eat-dog world," full of anger and death … and the Christian is not exempt. As the poet Tennyson put it, "nature red in tooth and claw."

BREAKING NEWS

Student Recounts Bullying

LIVE

Student details 'terrible' bullying at school where classmate committed suicide: 'I was terrified'

Student stayed home from high school for a week out of fear of being 'jumped'

While some struggle, some just deny reality. Even though we all see people dying around us every day, many of us have, at some level of our consciousness, convinced ourselves that this will not happen to us. In a way, we try to avoid reality in order to somehow think that we can get out of dealing with death. But when someone close to us dies, or there is a major tragedy like the destruction of the World

Trade Center in New York in 2001, we don't know how to deal with it. We sorrow for a while, but soon we shelve the issue again and get on with life.

In the long run, it doesn't help to deny. The issues will resurface in some way, at some time. Those who are most honest, yet have the fewest answers, seem to be at risk the most ... and sometimes they lash out in the process. Every day, anger and frustration boils over in our youth, sometimes with deadly force. A young man who shot and murdered his parents and two fellow high school students in Springfield, Oregon, wrote these words:

> It is easier to hate than love because there is so much more hate and misery in the world than there is love and peace. Look at our history — it's full of death, depression, rape, wars, and diseases.[3]

Are you beginning to see that "the question" is a big issue out there? How can there be a God of love? Look at all the hate. Look at all the awful things in the world. A loving, caring God must not exist. As Christians, if we are going to be consistent, we must be able to explain a world where we have joy and we have sorrow, a world where we have both life and death, both love and hate ... all at the same time. How do we do that? Reality seems so incompatible with the concept of a God of love. How do we explain it?

A question as important and as integrated as the one dealing with pain, suffering, and death cannot be answered superficially. Too many people offer answers with little sub-

---

3. Milton Keynes, *Salt Magazine* (for all ages), Scripture Union (UK), Jan./Mar. 1998, p. 29.

Arlington National Cemetery photo by Master Sgt. Jim Varhegyi, U.S. Air Force. Public domain, via Wikimedia Commons

stance and even less supporting evidence. I've even heard many Christians say something like, "We don't know why these horrible things happen, but we just need to trust God." But we do know why these things happen from a big picture perspective even if we don't understand every aspect of it all. To sufficiently address these critical issues of our existence, we must go in-depth, digging deep into the most essential foundations of our belief system. Our belief system is called a "worldview." And our worldview is built upon a foundation, either God's Word or man's word. This worldview constitutes the glasses through which we look at every aspect of reality. This determines how we interpret what we observe and experience and determines how we make decisions.

As we now address the question "If God is a good and loving God, why is there pain and suffering in the world?" it is absolutely essential that we first investigate the two main worldviews upon which people have built their answers. You'll soon see that these two worldviews are diametrically opposed to each other — and as you face difficult circumstances, these two worldviews will go to war with each other on the battlefield of your heart.

Time and Death

The secular-humanist worldview (sometimes called "man's view") begins with the assumption that physical matter is the only thing that exists. According to this view, everything that exists was formed at the "big bang," where all the matter in the universe appeared as a result of natural processes. (No one claims to know what caused this to happen, but they do claim that it happened and that's when space, mass, time, and the universe began.) Somehow, the matter that came from nowhere spontaneously arranged itself (with no outside influence or organization) into the first complex living cells over the course of billions of years and the random interaction of chemicals and molecules. Then, over the next hundreds of millions of years, these simple cells are believed to have "evolved" by natural processes into the forms we see today. That process of naturalistic evolution supposedly took place through chance genetic mutations and a process called "natural selection" in which only the "fittest" of organisms survive long enough to reproduce. Answers in Genesis provides many answers to questions about the topic of origins on our website and the hundreds of resources that are published. In this book, I am not covering this aspect in detail, but dealing with how a Christian can explain why we live in a world so permeated by death and suffering if there's a loving God.

The late Dr. Carl Sagan said, "The secrets of evolution are time and death."[1] He believed that the process of death and bloodshed, over millions of years, had the result of one kind of organism changing into another and eventually humans evolving from ape-like creatures. To try to categorize life and explain how evolution has progressed, secular scientists have attempted to create a "phylogenetic tree" that traces the history of life. In reality this is a "tree of death" because it is based on natural selection (where millions of organisms die over time), passing on to the next generation the supposed benefits of genetic mutation. (In most cases, however, genetic mutations weaken, rather than strengthen an organism … a fact that makes this belief mathematically impossible.)

Those who cling to the belief of evolution often appeal to circumstantial scientific "evidence" to attempt to prove their point — but I find time and time again that they are not motivated by the evidence at all. A proper interpretation of the same evidence (including an awareness of the most foundational laws of physics) leads one to conclude that matter and life must have been caused by an outside influence that both designed and created it. That "outside influence" confirms that there is a God, and what I observe is that many

---

1. Carl Sagan, "Cosmos, Episode #2: One Voice in the Cosmic Fugue," Public Broadcasting Service, 1980.

evolutionists object to the idea of God on moral or philo-sophical grounds first, and then attempt to disprove "God" with what they claim is science.

The moral/philosophical objection is often stated as the question "If God is all-powerful, loving, and merciful, why do we see children dying, people suffering, and bad things happening to good people? Is He not powerful enough to overcome it? Surely such suffering and evil means that either God is not powerful or good, or that He doesn't exist at all."

Many people have asked these questions with sincerity. Many have not been able to answer them sufficiently and have rejected the "idea of God," turning to the secular-hu-manist world view based on evolutionary beliefs as their new foundation for life. In response to painful and diffi-cult circumstance (often the untimely or painful death of a loved one, or an unjust personal abuse suffered) they begin to interpret everything in a way that attempts to disprove God's existence. While many origins debates with evolution-ists tend to focus on science and interpreting evidence, this is not always the true objection they have against God. Their arguments are usually fueled with passion and pain. Many lash out in great agony over a great loss or "injustice" in their personal lives; many feel neglected or abandoned by people, the church, or God Himself … and in many ways I'm sure we can relate. We have been there with all sorts of questions as we deal with tragedy, grief, and so on.

However, from their naturalistic evolutionary perspec-tive, why should they feel hurt (or anger) over the death or mistreatment of anyone? After all, in an evolutionary world, humans are of no more value than that of any other form of life. And how can anyone decide something is "just" or "unjust" if there's no absolute authority? Life ultimately then has no meaning or purpose, and when someone dies, from this perspective they cease to exist. So eventually everyone ceases to exist. So why does anything matter at all? And yet we all innately know that there's something wrong with death, injustice, and pain — and that human life really does matter.

My Brother

I loved my brother Robert. As an earthly brother and also as my brother-in-Christ, we had much in common, sharing the most important things life has to offer, the things that bond you together deeply. Both of us were in Christian ministry, teaching the Word of God. Over the years, we spent countless hours on the phone and in person discussing personal issues. We had grown together both physically and spiritually as children. Now as adults and fathers we continued to sharpen each other in our faith and in our family.

Robert (far left) as a young boy with his Mother and 4 siblings (1 more came later).

Robert (front) with 4 siblings.

My wife Mally was the first to begin to notice that something was changing over time — not changing in Robert, but in me. I was getting irritated. My regular telephone conversations with Rob were becoming a source of frustration and Mally picked up on this. "I don't understand," I would often say. "He is becoming so difficult to deal with." Our theological conversations began to degenerate into disjointed arguments, and it began to make me feel defensive and angry.

Others in the family began to notice something as well. Most concluded that Robert (like many pastors) was suffering from great stress resulting from his position and ministry. One day I received a very disturbing phone call from one of my friends. He faithfully attended Rob's church — even though he lived over an hour away — because he loved Rob's verse-by-verse Bible teaching. On this particular day, he had taken some of his visiting relatives to the church but was greatly disturbed because the sermon Rob gave seemed to lack logic and was very disjointed. He told me that the sermon basically didn't make sense.

Many in his congregation shared these feelings and some were beginning to take offense at his changing demeanor. Our phone conversations began to focus on the people who were leaving the church. Time after time Rob would tell me that another family had left. I couldn't understand what was happening. Those around him kept saying he was suffering from severe stress. That seemed to be a possible explanation, so eventually friends and family convinced Rob to take a break from the ministry and encouraged him to rest and recuperate.

But rest and recuperation never came. He wasn't getting better. We all realized something serious was wrong, but none of us were prepared for what was revealed after a barrage of tests over many months. At age 43, Rob was diagnosed with a degenerative brain disease for which there was no earthly cure. He would never again preach the Word of God as he had so loved to do.

On one level, the diagnosis made complete sense, solving a physical riddle that had perplexed us for quite some time. We finally knew what the problem was. But on another level, the diagnosis hit us like a tornado, causing our thoughts and our faith to be thrown about in a swirling, confusing cloud. Sure, we now knew what the problem was ... but now we had to face the question of why.

Why? Why would a loving and all-powerful God allow a dedicated man of God to be struck down in the prime of life? Why should he be subject to such a dreadful, dehumanizing disease — one that caused him to lose his mental faculties, his muscular function, his dignity? "But he was such a great preacher; he stood firmly on the Word of God; he preached the gospel; he wouldn't knowingly compromise God's Word," said my mother. "I still don't understand why God would allow this to happen to him!"

My breaking point was reached one day when I took Rob to a local shopping center. I thought this would be a simple outing, but it turned out to be one of those heart-gripping, emotional events that I'll never forget … one that has been indelibly impressed on my mind. By this time, the disease had taken quite a hold and he couldn't speak much. He was difficult to control and wanted to wander off and grab things out of the stores. Just dealing with this and watching a man who had been so upright in character do things we had to apologize for, was gut-wrenching. Only those who have lived through such a horrific ordeal can even begin to understand what families go through in such situations.

At the shopping center, Rob sat down with me to eat one of his favorite meals — Aussie meat pie and "mushy" peas. Suddenly, Rob saw some people in Muslim garb walking by. He jumped up and ran to them. "Wrong, wrong!" he shouted out. I gripped the table and held back my tears. Rob stared at the Muslims: they stopped and looked perplexed. "Wrong! Wrong!" he continued to say. Somewhere deep inside, Rob's soul still carried that burden to tell Muslims the truth about God — his heart still burned with the passion to see them come to know the forgiveness of Christ and be set free from the slavery of their religion. The passion for others and for God's Word that had directed his life was still intact, still driving him from within, but his brain could no longer communicate the message of the gospel that had been the focus of his preaching. "Wrong! Wrong!" was all he continued to shout. I ran to Rob, held him close, and apologetically led him away from the stunned Muslims and the gathering crowd. That's when "the question" became vividly real to me: why? Why, God? Why Robert? Why this way?

Back at the table, I did my best to regain some composure. We continued to eat our meat pie and mushy peas. Across from me sat my brother, a hollow shell of his former self. Why?

As I began to search for answers, my mind went back to our childhood. I saw vivid memories of the good times when we played together, those special days when our parents took us camping, the laughter and normal jostling that takes place between siblings. One doesn't usually think about death at that time of one's life. Even growing up as a teenager I had to attend a funeral or two, but it still didn't really hit me that this could happen to me or someone very close to me. The older I get, the more I have to deal with the death and suffering of people I have known and loved.

The issue of death and separation from a loved one or special friend really begins to hit home. The first time I had to face such a thing was when my father died . . . but my father died at what most would consider to be a more "appropriate" age — though 66 is still not that old in my books. Now I was facing the death of my brother, someone in the prime of life, someone younger in age than myself.

How was I to answer? It doesn't matter how dedicated a Christian we are, we struggle in these circumstances. Thankfully, during that critical season, I had something that many, many people don't: I had a heritage. I had been born and raised in a family that used God's Word as its final authority in all things. I had been taught and discipled that the Bible is the absolute authority of the Word of God and the foundation for my thinking (worldview) in every area. Through the example of my father and my experiences in the ministry of Answers in Genesis, I had also learned to think critically, to dissect and dismantle attacks against God and the Word.

Responding to the Objection

I need you to do a little thinking with me for a moment, for the problem of evil and suffering isn't just a personal one, it's also a philosophical one. The question is not only one of science, theology, and/or emotion. It's also a question of logic, so we will first respond with logic. The basic argument against the existence of God based on evil and suffering sounds like this:

> A good God would not allow or cause bad things to happen. Bad things happen. Therefore, God must not exist.

Now in order for this argument to have meaning, we must first consider the meaning of "good."

Matthew 19:16–17 addresses this very question:

> *And behold, a man came up to him, saying, "Teacher, what good deed must I do to have eternal life?" And he said to him, "Why do you ask me about what is good? There is only one who is good."*

In this passage, Jesus was challenging the man to realize the implications of what he had asked. Jesus pointed out that only an infinite being who is infinitely good should be called "good." Jesus' point is that God is good, and goodness is defined by Him.

I want you to think about this: Only the person who believes in God has a basis to make moral judgments to determine what is "good" and what is "bad." Those who claim that God does not exist have absolutely no authority upon which to call something right or wrong. If God doesn't exist, who can objectively define what is good and what is bad? What basis could there be to make such judgments? The atheist has no basis upon which to call anything good or bad. They can talk about good and bad, and right and wrong — but it's all relative, it's all arbitrary. What's "good" in one person's mind might be completely "bad" in another's.

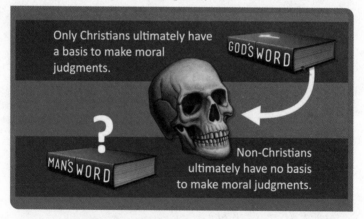

Only Christians ultimately have a basis to make moral judgments.

GOD'S WORD

?

MAN'S WORD

Non-Christians ultimately have no basis to make moral judgments.

So here is the point: For "good" and "bad" to exist, God must exist. The unbeliever does not, of course, accept that there is such a being. That means that when he makes the claim that a "good" God and "bad" things in this world cannot be reconciled, he cannot make the claim without assuming that God, indeed, does exist. If he doesn't, his argument falls apart!

In other words, the atheist has a big problem when he argues against God on the basis of "good" and "bad." Because in order for "good" and "bad" to exist, God must exist. The assumption that "good" and "bad" exist assumes that there is a God. Anyone who speaks of "good" and "bad" has to presuppose a worldview that includes God, because without a godly worldview there can be no absolute authority to define those words.

Christian apologist Greg Bahnsen stated it this way:

> Philosophically speaking, the problem of evil turns out to be, therefore, a problem for the unbeliever himself. To use the argument from evil against the Christian world view, he must first be able to show that his judgments about the existence of evil are meaningful, which is precisely what his unbelieving world view is unable to do.[1]

The bottom line is this: Arguments involving "good," "bad," "right," "wrong," etc. cannot be used to disprove the existence of God. Philosophically, they show that God does exist. Without an absolute authority, one can't ultimately determine what is "good," "bad," "right," or "wrong." This doesn't reconcile the problem of a good God co-existing with an evil world, but it does demolish the faulty logic that some use to dismiss God altogether.

When secularists decry the Bible's account of God sending the Israelites to war to kill all those in a particular city as "unjust," they have to borrow from the Christian worldview

---

1. G.L. Bahnsen, *Always Ready — Directions for Defending the Faith* (Nacogdoches, TX: Covenant Media Press, 2002), p.169.

to use such a term as "unjust." How can they accuse God this way? They can't! And what right do they have to say their "justice" is above that of God? If God truly is holy and just, He would have reasons for why He commanded the Israelites to do this (such as these cities being filled with wickedness and sexual perversion, like Sodom and Gomorrah were; see Genesis 15:16). God is the absolute authority and created everything and therefore has the right to do whatever He wants. And He knows the heart of every person, we don't. As Abraham said leading up to the judgment on Sodom and Gomorrah, *"Shall not the Judge of all the earth do what is just?"* (Genesis 18:25).

Actually, there is no good answer to the question that asks, "How could a good God exist when there is so much bad in the world?" There is no good answer because it's a bad question to begin with! It's called a "self-defeating" argument. There is a much better question that must be addressed — and we will do so shortly. But first, let's consider the tragic consequences of dismissing God on these grounds.

Meaninglessness

The secular-humanist worldview has no answer to the questions concerning the problems from evil and suffering. In fact, it has no answer to much of anything. In a world without God, everything must have happened just by chance random processes. There was no intent, no design, no purpose … it all "just happened." In such a world, there is no true meaning to anything. Life is tough, and then you die. Period.

Dr. Richard Dawkins is an atheist and one of the world's leading spokespersons for atheistic evolution. An interviewer once made this statement to him: "The idea of evolution and natural selection makes some people feel that everything is meaningless, people's individual lives and life in general." Dr. Dawkins responded, "If it's true that it causes people to feel despair. That's tough. If it's true, it's true; and you had better live with it."[1] So if one believes in atheistic evolution and it causes that person to despair, what can they do? Be tough. Get used to it. That's what it's all about. Live with it.

And then he was asked this question, "What do you see is the problem with a terminally ill cancer patient believing in an afterlife?" Dr. Dawkins responded, "No problem

---

1. Laura Sheahen, "The Problem with God: Interview with Richard Dawkins," interview conducted at the World Congress of Secular Humanism, October 2005, www.Beliefnet.com.

at all. If I could have word with a would-be suicide bomber who thinks he is going to paradise, I would say 'Don't imagine for one second that you are going to paradise, you're going to rot in the ground.'"[2]

Richard Dawkins
Photo by Steve Jurvetson; via Wikimedia,
CC BY 2.0; https://creativecommons.org/licenses/by/2.0/legalcode

At least Dr. Dawkins is consistent and honest. Without God, nothing matters. It doesn't matter if you are terminally ill or if you are a terrorist. You are going to die, and that is the end of it. Life, then, is utterly meaningless. Nothing you can do will make a difference. When you die, you won't even remember you were here, and in a short time, no one else will remember you either. Life has no meaning; it never did; it doesn't now; and it never will. It's just time and death. That's all. That's tough. Get used to it.

By the way, if what Dr. Dawkins is saying is true, why does he bother arguing against Christians or about anything? What's the point? Think about it! I have often wondered why an atheistic evolutionist would bother trying to convince someone of something. They believe that when you die

---

2. Ibid.

that's the end of you. Isaac Asimov believed that, Carl Sagan believed that, and that's what Richard Dawkins is saying. When you die, you rot, that's it. From that perspective, you won't even know you were ever here; you won't even know you ever existed. You won't remember any of it … and neither will anyone else; so therefore, what is the point of arguing with the creationists? I don't understand why they do argue against Christianity except that it's a spiritual issue.

I remember a man who came up to me after one of my talks at the University in Dublin in Ireland. He was fairly upset by the things I had taught and said, "When you are dead, you're dead! You prove to me there's life after death! When you're dead, you're dead!" I thought, "Well, I can't prove scientifically that there's life after death; true science just can't prove such things." So, I started to talk to him about some of the things I said in the lecture and what the Bible said. But he just kept saying, "When you're dead, you're dead. When you're dead, you're dead. When you're dead, you're dead!"

So finally, I got so frustrated I said, "Well, if that's it, when you're dead, you're dead, you won't even know you existed, won't even know you were ever alive, you won't even remember this conversation … you won't even know you were here. You won't know anything so it's as if you never existed!" And then I told him "You may as well go and jump off a cliff right now!" And he said, "You know what, I may as well, just to show you!" And I thought, "Uh oh. Now I've done it. This person is going to do himself in because of my lecture!" Well, we both settled down a little and talked some more. And you know what? He came back to the seminar the next night and asked me for a book about God.

It's an odd situation when you think about it. The Bible says that everyone knows in their heart that God exists as He has made this plain to all, and yet so many try in futility to "disprove" Him. Romans 1:20 states that *For his invisible attributes, namely, his eternal power and divine nature, have been clearly perceived, ever since the creation of the world, in the things that have been made. So they are without excuse.*

The atheist claims that because of "bad" things, a "good" God cannot exist ... but in the process, he must assume that God does exist. The atheistic evolutionist claims that life has no meaning and that there is no "truth," and yet many of them have devoted their lives to convincing others that their point of view is true. The man in Dublin claimed that "when you're dead, you're dead," yet he came back again with the hope that maybe there would be life after death after all.

So again, let me assure you that the secular-humanist worldview has no answer for the problems of suffering and death ... and in times of trouble, they not only face complete meaninglessness in the circumstances, but they also have nowhere to look (other than themselves) for strength. I must say, I often wonder how a non-Christian can even begin to cope in situations like the one our family had found itself in. For such a person, this life, as far as they believe, is all there is. When a loved one dies, they believe that is the end of them — they exist no more. How they must despair. But surely, it must even be more despairing to think that if this life is all there is, then even the few years we have are utterly meaningless. No wonder Paul says in 1 Thessalonians 4:13, *But we do not want you to be uninformed, brothers, about those who are asleep, that you may not grieve as others do who have no hope.*

The Right Question

I hope you are beginning to realize that a deep question cannot be resolved with a superficial answer. It should be clear by now that the worldview we have, and the foundation it is built upon, ultimately determines the course of our thoughts.

As we look at the secular-humanist worldview, we see it is based on the wrong foundation of man's word, so the resulting interpretation of evidence is also faulty. Because of this, any conclusions are therefore based on faulty logic ... logic that leads to a meaningless, futile existence. Because non-Christians have been indoctrinated to believe that our existence is the result of nothing more than time and death (millions of years of suffering, disease, bloodshed, and death), they are not going to understand about a God of love until they begin to see life through a true, uncompromised Christian worldview with the correct foundation of the timeline of history from Genesis 1–11.

So, we have yet to find an answer to the death and suffering issue for the secular worldview has none to offer. As Bible-believing Christians, however, we begin with a totally different foundation. We begin with the fact that a good God does exist and the history of life and the universe He has revealed to us is true. Through the witness of the inerrant Scriptures, a right interpretation of scientific fact, and the understandings that God has placed in our hearts, we can presuppose a Christian worldview that says God is there.

From there we can now ask the right question: How do you explain death and suffering in a world where an all-powerful, loving, and just God exists? That's the question believers wrestle with, isn't it? We know that God is, and we know that He is good. Desperately, we seek reconciliation between the pain and evil we see and this loving God we believe in.

Thankfully, when we start with the Bible, beginning with Genesis for answers, and let His Word speak for itself, that reconciliation takes place both in the mind and in the heart.

Now what we are going to find is that the only way to begin to come up with answers is by building our worldview on the literal history of Genesis 1–11, in particular the first three chapters that outline the origin of sin and death.

But here is a major problem. The majority of church leaders have either not taught much about Genesis 1–11, or claim it's not that important, or have compromised the Genesis account of origins to accommodate evolutionary/ millions of years beliefs. This is one of the reasons why so many Christians don't know how to correctly understand and deal with issues, such as death and suffering.

Genesis 1–11 relates the history in geology, biology, astronomy, anthropology, paleontology, and more that is the key to everything! It's this history in Genesis 1–11 that is foundational, not just to understanding the physical world around us, but also to the rest of the Bible, to all doctrine, to the gospel, to the Christian worldview, and, in fact, to everything. To understand marriage, one has to start with

Genesis 1–11, where we read God created marriage (Genesis 2:24). To deal with gender, one has to start with Genesis 1–11 where we read God made two genders, male and female (Genesis 1:27). To deal with racism, one has to start with Genesis 1–11 where we read God created all people from one man and one woman so we're all one race. I have dealt with the foundational importance of Genesis 1–11 in much more detail in my books *Divided Nation: Cultures in Chaos and a Conflicted Church* and also *The Lie: Evolution*.

Suffice it to say, if a Christian wants to understand how to resolve the issue of death, suffering, and disease permeating this world with belief in a God of love, then we have to start with Genesis 1–11 and build our thinking, our worldview, upon what is revealed to us in these chapters. Once we have the right foundation and the right worldview, we can

then begin to look at this world through that worldview and
start to unravel this seemingly irresolvable problem.

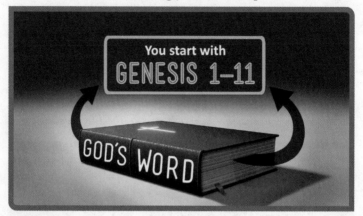

The Big Picture

Throughout Europe, many of the great cathedrals and castles of the world still stand tall today, marking an era of human history and creativity unique and unmatched: the Renaissance. Some of these magnificent structures date to medieval times, just before the Renaissance. While decorated with gold and elaborate tapestry, among the most impressive elements of their construction are the artistic images that often begin underfoot, span the walls, and then arch across the ceilings. From a distance, they flow seamlessly from scene to scene, displaying in glowing detail the stories and likenesses that the artist sought to record. From up close, however, an unbelievable reality emerges: these massive works of art are actually mosaics; consisting of millions — hundreds of millions — of minute, single-colored tiles, each placed one-by-one over the course of decades. The closer you are, the more the tiles themselves dominate your vision … and the harder it is to see how the pieces fit into the larger work. When you are very close, you can't tell at all what you are looking at … the tiles look like a random and senseless assortment of pieces.

That's where I found myself in the winter of 2000. As I struggled to answer the questions about what was happening to my brother, I found that I was too close to the situation to see clearly; my heart was too near the pain to make sense

Basilica of San Vitale, Italy by Petar Milošević.

of what was going on. That's when I knew I needed to stand back and begin to look at what was happening from a bit of a distance. In the midst of the difficult details of what we were facing, I needed to put things in the context of the "big picture."

For years, I've been committed to the "big picture." Starting with the Word of God, its history, and its principles, I've always sought to build a consistent worldview based on Scripture. This worldview is a framework of sorts; a grid of truth that can then be used to analyze the specific situations and the "evidence" we see around us. It's like putting on a pair of glasses — a pair of biblical worldview glasses. In that way, I've always tried to present a broad, biblical view in regard to issues that really affect our culture. Just like a mosaic, viewing the larger perspective allows us to see the details for what they are, and they then find meaning in the sum of the whole picture. The true biblical "big picture" encompasses a Christian worldview that begins with that foundation history of Genesis 1–11 — Creation (Genesis 1–2), Corruption (Genesis 3), Catastrophe (6–9), Confusion (Genesis 11) — and then on to Christ, Cross, and Consummation (what we at AiG, and in our Creation Museum, call the 7 C's of History). An understanding of the entirety of human history — the past as well as what is prophesied for the future — allows us to properly place ourselves within it, seeing more clearly what might appear to be random, unexplained events.

At this point, it's important that you know that simply because you are a Christian doesn't mean that you have a Christian worldview. In fact, very few Christians see the world correctly. Statistics indicate that less than 6% of American

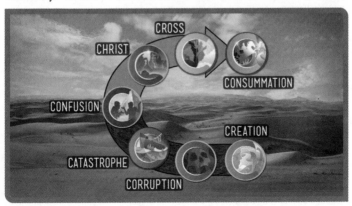

Christians have a biblical worldview,[1] and only 6% of Christian schools here in the United States teach a true Christian worldview.[2] Many of us have been indoctrinated to believe in some sort of mixture of the secular humanist worldview and the biblical one. Even though they might believe in Christ as their Savior, they might also believe in Darwinian evolution and that there were millions of years of suffering and death in nature before man supposedly evolved. Even though they believe in a God of love, they can't respond adequately to the questions of the non-Christian. When difficult times come, a Christian who adheres to the worldly perspective of human history and origins suffers from confusion over reality, finding themselves without an awareness of the true "big picture" that enables them to begin to make sense out of the detail.

From my experience, because most Christians have been educated in the public education system, and because most churches have not taught Genesis as they should, most really have a predominantly secular worldview which they have "Christianized."

I find most Christians really don't understand worldview. But it's vital to understand worldview, because your way of thinking doesn't come out of the air! Rather, it's like the structure of a house — it has to have a foundation. As

---

1. Nicole Alcindor, "George Barna says most Americans blend beliefs together as 'customized worldview': 'Nation in crisis,' " The Christian Post, September 21, 2022, https://www.christianpost.com/news/george-barna-says-most-americans-have-a-customized-worldview.html.

2. Stats are from a letter to Mark Looy from the Nehemiah Institute, Inc., November 26, 2021 on file at AiG

I've said earlier, if our thinking is not built on the foundation of an historical Genesis 1–11, we will not have a true biblical worldview.

No wonder Christianity seems to have lost its power! Christians have lost biblical Christianity, which is based on the Word of the living God beginning in Genesis. It's only when the Christian understands the biblical origin of death and suffering that they will be able to give an answer to both the non-Christian and to themselves. Developing a Christian worldview is vital ... and it is a process, as Paul points out in Romans 12:2: *Do not be conformed to this world, but be transformed by the renewal of your mind, that by testing you may discern what is the will of God, what is good and acceptable and perfect.*

Nowhere is this more important than in dealing with this seemingly perplexing and often painful question regarding the cause of suffering and death. Scripture has the answer to this problem ... and it's an answer that silences the skeptic and gives comfort and perspective to the perplexed and hurting Christian. But to find it, one must be willing to accept what the Bible says, and often cut through much religious and worldly heresy that has infiltrated the church. Without a correct historical timeline of events, little of this makes sense. So, let's stand back and begin to build the big picture of history.

Before time and space as we experience it, there was God. He is an all-powerful God (Jeremiah 32:17, 27), an eternal God without beginning or end (1 Kings 8:27; Isaiah 57:15), and a God who knows all (Isaiah 48:3–5; 1 John 3:20). He exists in eternity. He's a merciful and gracious God. Scripture even says that the mercy of the Lord is from everlasting to everlasting (James 5:11; 1 Peter 1:3). He is also a God that loves (John 3:16) and actually is love (1 John 4:7–8).

When God created reality as we know it, He did so in six literal days as recorded in Genesis 1, and when He was done, He said that everything He had made was *very good*. In fact, if you look up this word in the original Hebrew, the translation should really be that it was "exceedingly good."

It's appropriate to dwell on that for a moment. What God originally made exceeded good. I believe it was so good that we really can't imagine what it was like at all! Can you imagine a world that was perfect? Functioning in absolute harmony? Where man and woman walked in complete intimacy with their Creator?

I can't imagine that kind of goodness; yet our earth was such a world. Even among the animal kingdom, death and disease were unknown. Originally, the animals were vegetarian, and man was vegetarian as well (Genesis 1:29–30). Now some Christians claim there was death in the original world God made as plants were eaten for food, and therefore plants died. Yes, plants were eaten, but Scripture itself makes an important distinction between plants and animals. In Genesis 1, we see a general Hebrew term — *nephesh*. This word refers to living creatures such as man and animals. The word doesn't apply to plants, but it does apply to animals. The Bible clearly distinguishes between animals that have a *nephesh* and the plants which do not. So, the Bible would not classify plants as living creatures in the same way as those that have blood and flesh. In fact, God's Word states, *For the life of the flesh is in the blood* (Leviticus 17:11).

To understand this more, let us consider the definition of *die*. The following explanation is found in an article on the Answers in Genesis website:

> We commonly use the word *die* to describe when plants, animals, or humans no longer function biologically. However, this is not the definition of the word *die* or *death* in the Old Testament. The Hebrew word for *die* (or *death*), *mût* (or *mavet* or *muwth*), is used only in relation to the death of man or animals with the breath of life, not regarding plants. This usage indicates that plants are viewed differently from animals and humans.
>
> What is the difference between plants and animals or man? For the answer we need to look at the phrase *nephesh chayyah*. *Nephesh chayyah* is used in the Bible to describe sea creatures (Genesis 1:20–21), land animals (Genesis 1:24), birds (Genesis 1:30), and man (Genesis 2:7). *Nephesh* is never used to refer to plants. Man specifically is denoted as *nephesh chayyah*, a living soul, after God breathed into him the breath of life. This contrasts with God telling the earth on day 3 to bring forth plants (Genesis 1:11). The science of taxonomy, the study of scientific classification, makes the same distinction between plants and animals.
>
> Since God gave only plants (including their fruits and seeds) as food for man and animals, then Adam, Eve, and all animals and birds were originally vegetarian (Genesis 1:29–30). Plants were to

be a resource of the earth that God provided for the benefit of *nephesh chayyah* creatures — both animals and man. Plants did not "die," as in *mût*; they were clearly consumed as food. Scripture describes plants as *withering* (Hebrew *yabesh*), which means "to dry up." This term is more descriptive of a plant or plant part ceasing to function biologically.[3]

The death of creatures with nephesh has a very different impact on us as humans than the "death" of a plant.

Imagine you are out in the mountains and see the form of a large tree stump, twisted and weathered, bleached by the sun. You might look at this dead tree and think, "Wow, that is beautiful." Indeed, we even decorate our homes with dead and dried plants! But what would the neighbors think if you decorated with the dead, rotting carcass of a cow or something? (That's very different to taxidermy which are specially preserved skins). Or if you were in the woods and saw the decaying remains of an elk, would you think, "Wow, nice. Let's stop here and sit on this dead elk for the picnic!" No — but you might very willingly set up your

---

3. https://answersingenesis.org/biology/plants/do-leaves-die/.

picnic on a tree stump. There's something very different about animal death, isn't there?

Originally, there was no death or disease for those who had *nephesh*. In Genesis 1:29–30 we read:

> And God said, "Behold, I have given you every plant yielding seed that is on the face of all the earth, and every tree with seed in its fruit. You shall have them for food. And to every beast of the earth and to every bird of the heavens and to everything that creeps on the earth, everything that has the breath of life, I have given every green plant for food." And it was so.

Even though only plants were eaten as part of God's original creation, it wasn't until Genesis 9:3 — after the Flood — that God said to Noah, *Every moving thing that lives shall be food for you. And as I gave you the green plants, I give you everything.*

So, God made a change to man's diet so meat could be eaten. But that's not the way it started. Originally, it was a beautiful world. It was exceedingly good. Pain, suffering, disease, and death did not exist, and Adam and Eve walked freely with their God, uncovered and not ashamed in any way.

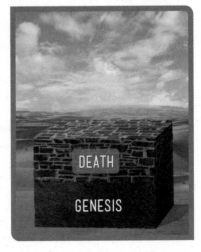

But then, it became corrupted, all of it. What happened? How did we get to the place we are at today? In Genesis, we again find the historical account of the actions that have led to our present realities of a death, suffering, and disease permeated world.

> *And the LORD God commanded the man, saying, "You may surely eat of every tree of the garden, but of the tree of the knowledge of good and evil you shall not eat, for in the day that you eat of it you shall surely die"* (Genesis 2:16–17).

The command was clear, and the implications were obvious. A line had been drawn and mankind was instructed to obey God's Word. But soon enough, Satan, the father of lies, would twist the command with a subtle deceit, with a half-truth that would cause Eve to question the intent of the command, appealing to the same desire we each face every day:

> *But the serpent said to the woman, "You will not surely die. For God knows that when you eat of it your eyes will be opened, and you will be like God, knowing good and evil"* (Genesis 3:4–5).

At that pivotal moment in history a choice was made that altered the course of humanity, sending shock waves forever into the future, spreading lies, pain, isolation, death, disease, and suffering to all generations.

> *So when the woman saw that the tree was good for food, and that it was a delight to the eyes, and that the*

tree was to be desired to make one wise, she took of its fruit and ate, and she also gave some to her husband who was with her, and he ate (Genesis 3:6).

The implications of their disobedience were immediate and obvious: A sense of guilt and nakedness overcame them, and they hid from the One who had made them. Philip Yancey described it this way:

> By their choice they put distance between themselves and God. Before, they had walked and talked with God. Now when they heard his approach, they hid in the shrubbery. An awkward separation had crept in to spoil the intimacy. And every quiver of disappointment in our own relationship with God is an aftershock from their initial act of rebellion.[4]

Next came the blame game. When God confronted them, Adam pointed the finger at Eve and Eve pointed to the serpent, each attempting to dodge the responsibility for what they had done. But it was too late, the damage had been done. Forever, humanity would be born into a cursed and broken world; one filled with pain and hardship — and at the end of it all we face the certainty of death:

> *"By the sweat of your face you shall eat bread, till you return to the ground, for out of it you were taken; for you are dust, and to dust you shall return"* (Genesis 3:19).

Throughout Scripture, the Bible points to this event, called the "fall" of man, as the origin of death, disease, and suffer-

---

4. Philip Yancey, *Disappointment with God* (Grand Rapids, MI: Zondervan, 1992), p. 61–62.

ing. In Romans 5:12, for example, Paul states, *Therefore, just as sin came into the world through one man, and death through sin, and so death spread to all men because all sinned.*

In Romans 6:23 he asserts that *the wages of sin is death*, and in 1 Corinthians 15:56 we read *the sting of death is sin.*

Here we see one of the great contrasts between the secular-humanist worldview, which claims that reality has evolved through "time and death" (over millions of years), and the biblical worldview that shows life in this fallen world was created but is permeated by sin and death. And it's important to understand from a Christian perspective that God is not to blame for death, disease, and suffering — we humans are because we in Adam sinned (committed high treason) against our Holy Creator God.

Not only does sin account for the separation we experience with God and the origin of death, but it also accounts for the decay and destruction we see in nature. Romans 8:22 tells us that *For we know that the whole creation has been groaning together in the pains of childbirth until now.* We now live in a groaning world of death, suffering, and disease because of our sin in Adam. The world we live in is not the same as the original world God made and declared was "very good."

For example, when we look at something like a tsunami, we could rightly call it a "sinami," because it is a natural consequence of Adam's disobedience. When Adam sinned, it sent shock waves through the entire universe, including nature. The covenant relationship between Adam and God was broken, as was the covenant relationship between Adam and the creation! In the beginning, God had placed man in dominion over creation, giving us the authority to subdue it.

But now, the creation is in rebellion against man, often with deadly consequences. So, dominion will now be an enormous battle.

Please understand the implications of this: It's not God's fault there's death, disease, and suffering in the world. It's our fault. And just like Adam, we would much rather point to someone else, or something else, rather than take responsibility for it ourselves. There is a remnant of beauty and a shadow of goodness on this planet, but when we look at all the horrible things going on, we don't want to admit that we are the ones who are to blame. We want to accuse somebody else. We want to blame God, or politicians, or our parents … always pointing elsewhere, rather than face the fact that we are dead in our own trespasses and sin.

Jeremiah 17:9 states that *The heart is deceitful above all things, and desperately sick* [wicked]. But instead of us saying, "Look what our sin did to the world!" you know what we want to say? "Why does God do that?" We don't want to admit the horrible thing that we did (and continue to do) when we sin. When we disobey, we are truly committing high treason against the God of creation. Do you realize how bad that sin is? Just look at what it has done to the world! Rather than shaking our fists at the heavens, we should be falling down on our knees in prayer, as Paul did, crying out,

Wretched man that I am! Who will deliver me from this body of death? (Romans 7:24).

Let us just stand back and ponder who God is: God is holy. Moses and the people sang a song in Exodus 15, exclaiming in verse 11, *Who is like you, O LORD, among the gods? Who is like you, majestic in holiness, awesome in glorious deeds, doing wonders?*

I really don't think we comprehend what it means that God is holy. As sinful, fallible human beings I believe this is beyond our comprehension. We need to understand as much as possible what sin did to the relationship between mankind and God. Think about it this way: when a loved one dies, we feel a terrible separation. The grief from that separation is awful. To me, this reminds us just a little of the separation between us and God because of our sin — and that separation is far greater. I am reminded of this when I think about the prophet Isaiah telling the Israelites how their many sins have separated them from God: *but your iniquities have made a separation between you and your God* (Isaiah 59:2). I think this helps a little in understanding that sin separates us from God.

God is holy! But God wants us to spend eternity with Him. However, as sinners we can't live with a holy God. That's why God had a plan to redeem mankind so we can spend eternity with our Creator. God Himself paid the penalty for our sin through His Son and His death and Resurrection. Now through the Son's redeeming work, God offers us the gift of salvation — it's free. Now we can come before our Father God, through His Son. God states about our righteousness:

> *We have all become like one who is unclean, and all our righteous deeds are like a polluted garment. We all fade like a leaf, and our iniquities, like the wind, take us away* (Isaiah 64:6).

But because of what Christ did, for those who receive the gift of salvation, God now sees us through Him.

The Bible states in Hebrews 9:22, *without the shedding of blood there is no forgiveness of sins*. Because death (physical as well as spiritual) was the penalty for sin, then there must be the giving of life to pay the penalty for sin. In Leviticus 17:11 we read, *For the life of the flesh is in the blood, and I have given it for you on the altar to make atonement for your souls, for it is the blood that makes atonement by the life*. So, in God's system of justice, He requires the shedding of blood, the giving of life to pay penalty for sin.

Now we as finite fallible humans can't ultimately answer why all this is so, except God who created us and owns everything requires it. God's Word tells us that God, who is the absolute authority, is totally just in all His ways.

> *The Rock, his work is perfect, for all his ways are justice. A God of faithfulness and without iniquity, just and upright is he* (Deuteronomy 32:4).

> *Righteousness and justice are the foundation of your throne* (Psalm 89:14).

We also need to be reminded that *"My thoughts are nothing like your thoughts," says the LORD. "And my ways are far beyond anything you could imagine"* (Isaiah 55:8; NLT). We will never be able to understand God's ways. That's why there is always a faith aspect, *And without faith it is impossible to please him, for whoever would draw near to God must believe that he exists and that he rewards those who seek him* (Hebrews 11:6).

So, because of man's rebellion (sin), God set up the sacrificial system to point to the one who would be the ultimate sacrifice, *And the LORD God made for Adam and for his wife garments of skins and clothed them* (Genesis 3:21). As well as the origin of clothing, this is the first blood sacrifice as a covering for their sin. But God's Word also teaches *For it is impossible for the blood of bulls and goats to take away sins* (Hebrews 10:4).

A man (Adam) brought sin and death into the world, so a man would need to pay the penalty for sin. You see, man was made in the image of God — no animal was made in God's image and animals are not connected (related) to human

beings. So, the shedding of an animal's blood and the giving of an animal's life can't take away our sin — a man must pay the penalty for sin.

Now a sinner can't pay the penalty for sin. And yet all humans are descendants of Adam which means that all humans are sinners, as Romans 3:23 states, *for all have sinned and fall short of the glory of God.* That's why all humans are under the judgment of death as Romans

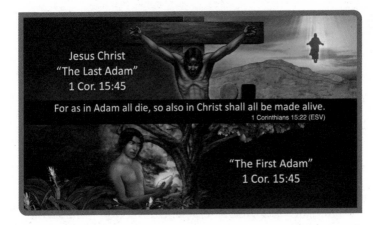

5:12 makes clear, *Therefore, just as sin came into the world through one man, and death through sin, and so death spread to all men because all sinned.* To pay the price for our sin, a perfect man was needed. That's why God stepped into history in the person of His Son, to become Jesus Christ the Godman, a member of the human race but sinless, so He could shed His blood and give His life to pay the penalty for sin. The first sacrifice in Genesis 3:21 is really a picture of what was to come in Jesus Christ being the ultimate sacrifice, *For the death he died he died to sin, once for all* (Romans 6:10).

> *For our sake he made him to be sin who knew no sin, so that in him we might become the righteousness of God* (2 Corinthians 5:21).

So, through the first man Adam came sin and death, and through the last Adam came life through death:

> *The first man Adam became a living being; the*

last Adam became a life-giving spirit (1 Corinthians 15:45).

For as by a man came death, by a man has come also the resurrection of the dead. For as in Adam all die, so also in Christ shall all be made alive (1 Corinthians 15:21–22).

Now consider this. From what we read in Scripture, angels are all individual creations. They don't marry and don't reproduce. God made two humans but made them flesh and blood so they can reproduce. Adam was the head of the human race. Adam represented all who would come from him. Adam was also given dominion over the creation. So, when Adam fell (sinned), all humanity then would be sinners, and the whole creation fell as Romans 8:22 states clearly.

For we know that the whole creation has been groaning together in the pains of childbirth until now.

Because humans have physical bodies, God could place upon us the judgment of death so our bodies would die.

For we know that the whole creation has been groaning together in the pains of childbirth until now.
Romans 8:22 (ESV)

However, as humans are made in the image of God, our soul will live forever.

> *And just as it is appointed for man to die once, and after that comes judgment* (Hebrews 9:27).

But as sinners we can't live with a holy God. God sent His Son to become a member of the one human race, so He could die and pay the penalty for sin and offer a gift of salvation to those who will receive it. The condition our body is in now could not stand the glory of heaven as, *flesh and blood cannot inherit the kingdom of God, nor does the perishable inherit the imperishable* (1 Corinthians 15:50).

God provides a priceless gift for us to receive:

> *because, if you confess with your mouth that Jesus is Lord and believe in your heart that God raised him from the dead, you will be saved* (Romans 10:9).

If God didn't place upon mankind the judgment of death, then humans would live in their sinful state forever. Now think about what sin has done to man as we read in Jeremiah 17:9, *The heart is deceitful above all things, and desperately sick; who can understand it?* We can't even comprehend man in his depraved state living forever. God wants us to spend eternity with Him. So He placed upon us the judgment of death so He could redeem us. That is simply awe-inspiring. We can't imagine how great God's love is that He would do that for us. This then makes sense of what God says in Psalm 116:15, *Precious in the sight of the LORD is the death of his saints.* God wants that separation to end and provided the way for that to happen.

As sinners, we deserve nothing. We in Adam rebelled against our Creator. We forfeited our right to live. God had every right to annihilate us. But — *For God so loved the world, that he gave his only Son, that whoever believes in him should not perish but have eternal life* (John 3:16).

So really, in judging us with death, God provided a way for Him to offer us a gift of salvation.

We need to be reminded again that death and this groaning world is a result of our sin. It's not God's fault. We can't rightly get angry at God but should be angry at our sin.

Responsibility lies with each of us and with all of us. Isaiah 59:1–2 restates the corruptive and divisive implications of sin in different words:

> *Behold, the LORD's hand is not shortened, that it cannot save, or his ear dull, that it cannot hear; but your iniquities have made a separation between you and your God, and your sins have hidden his face from you so that he does not hear.*

And it all started that one day in Eden when Adam and Eve succumbed to the temptation to become like God. The rest is history, and because we are all descendants of Adam, his history is our heritage. In numerous places the Bible refers to us being "in Adam." When Adam sinned, we were all "in" Adam, and thus must suffer the consequences of his rebellious action against a Holy God. (And, of course, we have all individually taken part in that rebellion in our own lives, too.) Since that day, we have been given a death sentence from the point of fertilization … and like Adam, we are naturally inclined to deny it and try to shift the blame.

12

Making Sense of Suffering

As the days passed and Robert's body and mind continued a slow and steady destruction at the hands of his disease, this "big picture" presented in Scripture began to give me a perspective from which I could make sense of the suffering Robert was facing and the death that was at hand. Now, both the question and the answer were becoming very clear. How do you explain death and suffering in a world where an all-powerful, loving, and just God exists? You explain it with sin — Adam's sin and our personal sin.

For many, however, the truth about sin and death (and our personal responsibility for it) is not an acceptable answer. Yes, it's hard to face the truth sometimes, and many who don't want to face the message will try to undermine the messenger. In our case, in this contemporary world, that means that many who don't want to take responsibility for sin and its consequences will try to attack the truth at its source ... that source being the Word of God.

My brother was a devoted defender of the Bible. Robert also understood that the history in Genesis is foundational to the rest of Scripture — and foundational to a correct big picture of life, for all Christian doctrine is founded in the history in Genesis. Robert also believed that Genesis makes it plain that there was no death, bloodshed, or disease before sin, and that sin originated at "the Fall" and continues through our personal actions.

Robert so wanted to teach people God's Word and was continually searching for the best tools to help him do so. A year or so before he was stricken with this terrible disease, Rob excitedly told me about a Bible study program produced by a well-known Australian theological college. However, he was immensely saddened to find that this program compromised the Word of God in the Book of Genesis with evolutionary teaching.

Rob believed that the Bible could not in any way accommodate the notion that life had evolved over millions of years, as this Bible study program did. To do so would be to say that the Bible's words cannot be trusted, and that God is an ogre. Integral to the notion of evolution and millions of years is the idea that the fossil record — with its evidence of death, disease, suffering, and violence — was laid down millions of years before man came on the scene. But the Bible says that at the end of the

Robert — devoted defender of the Christian faith.

sixth day of creation — after finishing the creation of all living things including Adam and Eve— God described the creation as "very good" (Genesis 1:31).

As Rob once said to me during one of our phone calls, "If God said death, suffering, disease, and violence is 'very good,' then God is an ogre. No, God created a perfect creation that has been corrupted by sin. There is no way the billions of fossils could have been laid down before man. I believe you're right in saying that most of the fossils resulted from the Flood of Noah's day, not from millions of years of death prior to the sin of man."

He knew that it was the sin of the first man, Adam, which resulted in the judgment of death and the entrance of disease, suffering, and violence into the world. Yet the Genesis section of this Bible study program had adopted the secular worldview of time-and-death evolution, and this was extremely upsetting to Rob. He saw what this theological college had done as an attack on God's Word — and like our father, Rob hated compromise. He realized that if one could take man's fallible interpretation of the world and reinterpret the Bible accordingly in Genesis, then this could be done with any passage in the Bible. People could start questioning the Resurrection or the virgin birth. And after all, no scientist has seen anyone rise from the dead, so maybe this part of the Bible should be reinterpreted also!

As a devout defender of the Bible, Rob wrote to the president of the college and eventually visited him, challenging him personally concerning this matter. Here is a portion of that letter:

> If death came into this world as a result of Adam's sin, where is there place for the evolutionary process? The evolutionary process is a process of death and struggle. If we were simply guided by the Bible with no other influence, I have no doubt that the only conclusion that could be made would be that death came into the world as a result of sin … Obviously, we do not have all the answers in respect to the original creation, and certain questions remain as a result of the Fall. However, we must acknowledge that we are looking back at a perfect creation through fallen eyes, and our first and authoritative revelation must come from the words of Scripture.

So many people do not approach the doctrine of creation from Scripture first but allow theories and assumptions from certain fields of science to create a framework of thinking that is then taken to Scripture, instead of the other way around. When faced with an important issue, Rob would go immediately to the Bible, beginning with Genesis, and answer from there. Without the literal history in Genesis, Rob would not have had a consistent, logical answer; and he would have floundered in poor philosophy and unending confusion just as the secular-humanist does when faced with these questions.

Over the 40 plus years I've been in the creation apologetics ministry, I've found both those inside and outside the church struggle with understanding  how one could believe in a loving God when observing this world of death, disease, and suffering. It's so sad that so many Christian leaders have told people there's no problem with a Christian accepting the belief in millions of years. However, that would mean that the death, disease, and suffering observed today has been happening for millions of years before man.

The idea of millions of years in our present era came out of those in the late 18th and early 19th centuries who wanted to explain everything by natural processes. Thus, the idea that the fossil record was formed as a result of natural processes over millions of years, not by Noah's Flood, was popularized. Now for those who read the Bible, we know that after God had created all things, including the first two humans, he said everything was "very good." If one accepts the millions of years, this means God is describing all the death and disease (including diseases like cancer) seen in the fossil record as very good. Does it make sense that the God of the Bible would declare cancer "very good"? For a Christian to accept millions of years of history would mean God is responsible for all the death, disease, and suffering in the world. But God is not responsible — our sin is!

But let there be no surprises when the clear answers found in Scripture often cause a stir and are rejected by many. There is no quick-fix solution when it comes to countering more than a century of evolutionary/millions of years indoctrination. Absolute truth is divisive truth, separating darkness and light. The humanist knows this is where the real battle is being waged and they will reject us on this point incessantly. Because Christ is the truth, His ministry was divisive as well. He said, *Do not think that I have come to bring peace to the earth. I have not come to bring peace, but a sword. For I came to set a man against his father, and a daughter against her mother* … (Matthew 10:34–35). Truthful answers can only

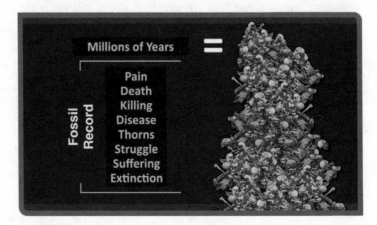

come from a truthful source. While many may not receive it, it is only from the source of truth, God's Word, that we can honestly find the foundational answers to the question regarding suffering and death. On the "big picture" foundation we can begin to build a clear understanding of our present circumstances. But without that foundation, what do we have to turn to?

The sincere believer in God, who seeks honest answers to the most perplexing and painful of life's problems, will find that the truth can set you free from the anger, disappointment, and futile hopelessness of the evolutionary worldview based on time and death. The biblical worldview (encompassing Creation, Corruption, Catastrophe, Confusion, Christ, Cross, and Consummation) gives the necessary perspective we need to face difficult realities even though we will not (and cannot) fully understand it all. That's why we must put our faith and trust in God's Word and not rely on our finite fallible human understanding.

The "big picture" sure helped me and my family as we wrestled with the questions about what was happening with my brother. How do you explain death and suffering in a world where an all-powerful, loving, and just God exists? The answer is sin. While this world had a perfect beginning, it was thrown into death and destruction by the willful choices of Adam and Eve to disobey the Father ... and we continue to sin day-to-day "in Adam."

As the issues we were facing began to take their place within the biblical worldview, I instinctively wanted to reach for the phone and call Rob to discuss these things with him, just as we had for years and years. What would he have to say? How would he apply the Word of God to this situation? As a pastor, how would he have counseled us, and what would he suggest we do in response to the circumstance we were in? I so desired to connect with him one more time. I longed for the opportunity to hear his perspective on what he himself was facing. But of course, as I looked at him now — just an empty shell of the former man he had been — I knew that was impossible ... or was it?

13

A Voice from the Past

As I returned to my room after visiting Rob in the nursing home, my mind was in high gear, still sorting out the implications of his illness. While the "big picture" put "the question" into a biblical framework, many other issues needed to be faced: What then should one expect out of life? Is this fair? Can God heal, and if so, why doesn't He? How do we help others in situations like ours?

Facing a serious illness and the certainty of the death of someone is a humbling experience … and one that wakes us up by shattering the illusion of security and health that surrounds us in the modern world. If you've walked the halls of a nursing home, you understand what I mean. If you or a loved one has been on the receiving end of a terminal medical diagnosis, you've felt it. If you've been to a funeral or two, you probably know what I'm talking about. In these moments — undistracted by the noise of the world — the reality that what the Bible says is true is seen with unusual clarity … and then usually quickly forgotten as one re-enters "regular" life. For many, when they have good health they, in a way, think this life just continues. When we're young, we tend not to even think about life being finite. And no matter how long we live on this earth (70, 80, 90, or so years), this is nothing compared to eternity! We need to let that sink in. And as hard as it is to do so because we have to live/suffer through circumstances, God's Word reminds us, *For I consider that the sufferings of this present time are not worth comparing with the glory that is to be revealed to us* (Romans 8:18).

I recall an interesting conversation I had with someone who was in the hospital after a horrific accident. This person had numerous serious injuries that would change him for life. He said how many people tried to comfort him by saying something like, "Just think, there's always someone worse off than you." He said to me, "I can't even imagine how bad the person who is the worst in the world must be." We need to recognize that it's easy to tell someone God is in control, or others are worse than you, but we live in this world and have to live through these circumstances. And sometimes they are terribly hard, painful, and agonizing. Yes, God is in control, but from a human perspective it is so hard for us to understand why such suffering happens.

As the realities of the inevitable loss of my brother intensified, so did my desire to connect with him again. Sure, I could talk to him (and did so as I sat at his bedside), but I was unable to tell if my words were getting through. At this point there was no response at all. How I yearned to hear his voice again; to discuss together what he — and we — were facing. But how could that happen? The very issue had placed a great gap between us, making it impossible for him to reach across the void that his illness had erected between him and the rest of us.

That's when my youngest brother gave me an audio recording on cassette tape.[1] "You've got to hear this," he

---

1. Cassette tapes were a popular way of recording audio in the past. In our modern era we mostly listen to audio recordings digitally on smartphones etc., or perhaps on CDs.

said. "It's almost prophetic." The label on the tape read *The Experience Trap, Robert Ham, June 1, 1997.* My mind did the math: This was a sermon that Rob had preached

only a couple of years before his major health issue began to manifest itself. "Rob deals directly with the very issue he's being confronted with right now," my brother continued excitedly. "It's like he's giving the sermon to himself!"

I was fairly stunned. What did he have to say that related to this current situation? Did he have some insight I hadn't been given that could throw more light on the situation? Could his words help his family or perhaps encourage others who are grieving over the pain and suffering of a loved one? Could this help us understand how to cope with his present condition? Might the historical and theological reconciliation I sought continue through the concise words of my brother, even as he lay with mumbled speech on his death bed? After looking at the tape for some time, I placed it in the cassette deck and pressed the "play" button....

> This morning, I want to address the issues of sin, sickness, and healing from the Word of God....

The health, vigor, and confidence of his words were startling — a complete contrast to who he had become. This was the brother I knew! This was the man whose desire to preach truth could be felt in the urgent intensity of his voice. As his message began to flow, I found myself clinging to every word. It was as if God had been preparing Rob, his family, and his friends for what was coming — answering ahead of time so many of the specific questions we were now facing.

As the tape rolled on, Rob's words began to speak alongside the Bible's words — the Word which he so deeply trusted and preached — and as they did, the context of the issues we were facing began to find reconciliation not only in my mind, but also in my heart.

Sure, I've taught the "big picture" in reference to geology, the family, and human history, but now, listening to Rob, I wasn't the teacher, I was the student: "You see, if there was no sin in the world ... there wouldn't be any sickness and there would be no death," he began. "There is not a person in this world who will not die.... Death is the ultimate 'sickness' that we all have to face as a result of sin."

When it came to the origin of sin and death, Rob and I were on the same page. We both understood from the Genesis narrative why there is suffering. Adam's rebellion in the Garden of Eden had corrupted the original creation and because we are all descendants of Adam and continue to sin, we all suffer the same problem. As he applied the "big picture" to the circumstances we were in — the circumstances he was in — many of the questions we were dealing with as he was slowly being destroyed by disease were answered in his own words — even as he now faced certain death.

Earlier in the day — the day my brother had given me the recording of Rob's sermon — I had been beside Rob's bed in the nursing home, holding his feeble hand. I kept thinking, "This is not normal, Rob. Surely it is not normal for this to happen to such a one as you." As I looked at his weakened body and his blank and sunken face (that had once been filled with the overflowing joy of his Christian character), I was overcome with the notion that this is not the way it should be, that his condition was not following the expected course of human life.

But that evening, Rob's own words on the tape countered my thoughts ... it was as if he knew back then what would be on my mind, and he used the example of the Apostle Paul to make his point:

> I am going to say this twice. I would like this to melt into your mind and into your heart. I want it to be written indelibly on your mind so that it will never, ever be wiped away. Please understand this. You see the Apostle Paul when we look at the whole New Testament. Paul saw illness and he saw sickness as normal. Let me spell it for you: N-O-R-M-A-L. I'd like to underline it with a great big felt pen and write it indelibly in every one of our minds. The Apostle Paul saw sickness and illness as normal living in a world ruined by sin. I'll say it again: the Apostle Paul saw illness and sickness as normal living in a world that has been ruined by sin.

Rob was right. We should expect illness and death. Although sickness is abnormal in the sense that it was not part of the original creation before sin, it should be considered "normal" in this fallen world. Had Rob been with us, helping us deal with his situation (looking on his disease-racked body and knowing the person lying there was a devout Christian) he would say, through tears of compassion, that this is the sort of thing to be expected in a sin-cursed universe. I believe Rob would then tell us that instead of focusing on the disease, we need to focus on Christ. As Rob continued to develop this part of his sermon on the tape, it became very clear to me what he would say to us now if he were able. I think it would be something like this:

> I know it's sad watching my body die and not being able to communicate with me. I know you feel a horrible separation but look at what the Bible says. It doesn't promise we will be physically healed in this sin-cursed world. Remember, we are all sick and dying because of sin — this is to be considered normal in this world. Even the people who were healed or raised from the dead by Christ during His earthly ministry or through the Apostles had only a temporary reprieve. Eventually, they had to die anyway. No one can escape this normal course of events for this world. But for the Christian, the wonderful news is that God does promise to comfort us and strengthen us, knowing we are sinful creatures living in such a fallen world. In Eden, our expectations could have been different. But now, outside the Garden, the consequences of sin dictate our destiny. While our unavoidable confrontations with illness and death will still pierce our hearts with grief, they should not come as a shock. As Peter counseled

the first generation of Christians, "Beloved, do not be surprised at the fiery ordeal among you, which comes upon you for your testing, as though some strange thing were happening to you…" (1 Peter 4:12; NASB).

Yes, illness and death is the norm in this post-Fall era of human history, and we should not expect otherwise.

But what about "original sin" and specific sins?

When trying to discern the root cause of illness, disease, and death, it's not uncommon for us to search out a particular sin that the suffering individual may have committed that has caused the problem. In his message, Rob explained that the consequences of certain sins could lead to sickness. (For example, alcohol abuse can lead to liver damage and unbiblical sexual behavior can lead to AIDS and a host of other very, very serious sexually transmitted diseases.) Also, there are times when God can cause people to become sick because of their rebellion against Him. Certainly, our specific sins can have their consequences in specific illnesses. As Galatians 6:7 says:

> Do not be deceived: God is not mocked, for whatever one sows, that will he also reap.

But, of course, there are other people who seem to have done nothing to cause their sickness (a baby born HIV positive, for example, or a child with leukemia). And then there are those who die in accidents or disasters that appear to have no direct connection to their personal sin at all. In those situations, the hardship may not be because of any specific sin in their life at all, but because of the sins of others or as a result of the world itself being fallen. Sin has been in the entire world since Adam and Eve rebelled. It is called "original sin," and it affects everyone.

Perceived innocence is no insulator against the all-encompassing effects of this sin. Every day bad things happen to good people ("good" as we might compare them to other "bad" people at least, but still sinful by God's standard!). These things come upon us because the world itself is fallen and the consequences of our sins "in Adam" which have been passed down through the generations.

As the audio recording rolled on, I realized that Robert had not only taught this truth with his words, but he was illustrating it with his own life, before my very eyes, as his mind and body continued their decline.

14

Isn't This All Very Unfair?

During one of my earlier visits to Australia, before Rob had deteriorated too badly, I took him on a trip to a country town west of Brisbane. He couldn't talk much and when he did, some of his sentences didn't make sense. He kept trying to tell me about his sermons — trying in some way to explain to me his unending love for preaching God's Word. He would say things like, "I did 14 on Genesis, and 10 on Romans and...." I figured that he was telling me about the sermons he had preached on those books, but nothing came out right. As he tried to speak, he seemed perplexed, and his face became as contorted as his words. No matter how hard he tried to explain, he couldn't say it. His memory that was once so full of knowledge concerning God's Word was basically gone. It was such a distressing and pitiful scene.

At this point, Rob could still play the piano and the accordion. We would motion to him to sit down at the piano or get out his accordion, and he would play with a big smile on his face; the music expressing the special talent the Lord had given him. Over time, though, this gift started to disappear. He could play fewer and fewer tunes, until he could play only parts of certain ones. Eventually, all his wonderful abilities in this area ceased.

After the disease had taken considerable control, we still took him to church — knowing that he wouldn't under-

Robert playing his piano accordion.

stand (as far as we knew) what was happening. It appeared as if he was still able to read … at least he would pick up his favorite books (especially the Bible) and seemingly read the words page after page (although we don't know how much, if anything, he understood). At one of the church services, we stood up to sing a hymn. Though Rob could no longer speak to us, he sang his heart out to the Lord with clear and convincing words. My mother, tears running down her cheeks, watched with breaking heart. But at the end of the service Rob did not seem to know anything about what he had done or what was going on around him.

Feelings of injustice overwhelmed us. Rob did everything because of his love for God and His Word. Now we were watching him die, and it was not just a "normal" death, but a slow, debilitating, and utterly dehumanizing one. It was horrible watching him being robbed of his ability to communicate and play the piano and accordion — the special gifts we believed God had given him — as his mental faculties left him. How incomprehensible it seemed to us to see his thoughts and speech, which he had so purposefully developed and used to communicate the gospel, now reduced to nothing. Why, Lord? It doesn't make sense, does it?

Sure, it all fit within the biblical framework, but it all seemed so unjust. During my lifetime, I've heard non-Christians mock God when they see a Christian suffering by saying such things as, "That person doesn't deserve to suffer like that. How can a God of love let someone who serves Him go through such a terrible situation?" Such mockery has made me really frustrated … but now we were asking the same questions. Sure, other "bad" people might deserve this kind of a death, but not a God-fearing servant like Rob, right?

I remember the day I received the devastating phone call. We had hoped his brain tests would come back negative; that was when we were still fairly sure that his problems were because of severe stress … at least that was our continued hope. However, the tests came back positive. Rob had a major problem — an unusual disease causing relentlessly progressive loss of brain function.

I didn't know what to say. My mind was in a daze. This couldn't be happening — not to Rob. Surely God wouldn't let this happen to a man who had sacrificed much to study and preach His Word? He had basically only just started his ministry — he was in the prime of life. At a time when there are so many Christian leaders who compromise the Word of God, and thus undermine its authority, my brother was totally committed to standing for its full authority. None of it seemed fair. I must admit that from an up-close human perspective, none of this seemed to make sense. Granted, Rob was a sinner (like all of us) … but not horrendous kinds of sins, not the kinds of sins that we see in the lives of lawless pagans — who often live long, carefree, and healthy lives. He was a man who sought God. Not only had he trusted the Lord Jesus Christ (the Creator of the universe) for salvation, but he had also dedicated his life to preaching God's Word.

Even though Rob, like everyone else, was under the condemnation of death, surely a God of love wouldn't let some terrible disease inflict a person like him? How could that be fair? Here was my brother, one of God's faithful children, afflicted with a disease most of us don't even want to think about — a disease that caused him to lose his mind and die slowly, while others lived on in health. My struggles echoed those of David, who in Psalm 73:12–14 said:

> *Behold, these are the wicked; always at ease, they increase in riches. All in vain have I kept my heart clean and washed my hands in innocence. For all the day long I have been stricken and rebuked every morning.*

Fueled by frustration and feelings, these thoughts were tossed around in my mind. But as I continued to stand back and see the big picture (putting our specific situation into the broader biblical perspective), I was led to a conclusion that reflected God's perspective rather than my human one. Did Rob deserve to suffer the way he did? But then we can ask this sort of question over and over again. Did that young Christian lady deserve to have miscarriages when the pagan couple down the street have lots of healthy kids? Did that wonderful Christian couple deserve to lose their son in a tragic accident? Did that Christian family with young children deserve to lose their mother to cancer? These questions and examples are basically endless. It's totally understandable to ask such questions as we have lived through these situations. But we are looking at them totally from a human perspective. In a sense, we are saying we don't deserve this.

So do any of us deserve to suffer like this? The answer is actually "yes."

When you think about it from a Christian perspective, we all deserve much, much more than the suffering afflicting Rob. Because of our rebellious condition, we don't even deserve to live. But God didn't annihilate us, He has allowed us to live — while at the same time giving us a taste of what life is like without God. We sin because we want independence from God; we want to be our own god. That was the hook of the temptation in the Garden: Eat of the fruit and you shall be like God. That alone should have been a complete and immediate death sentence for Adam (or for us as we make similar choices). If God didn't show merciful restraint, rather than fully granting our desire to be free from Him, we wouldn't even exist. Colossians 1:16–17 says:

> For by him all things were created, in heaven and on earth, visible and invisible, whether thrones or dominions or rulers or authorities — all things were created through him and for him. And he is before all things, and in him all things hold together.

God has obviously withdrawn some of that sustaining power

so that creation is no longer held in a perfect state but sustained in an imperfect state. Now our bodies and everything around us fall apart eventually. We are actually living in a world where we have a small taste what it is like to live without God — mutations, death, suffering, etc. This is a necessary consequence of rebellion against our Creator. We do deserve what befalls us. We don't deserve what God has done for us. We don't deserve even the life we do have.

Every second of every day we live in a fallen world, and we can experience pain, suffering, and hardships. This should remind us every day of how bad sin is and what a terrible tragedy has occurred in this world and our lives because of us. Oh, woe is us. What have we done!

15

Why Doesn't He Heal?

Sometimes, when I called my mother to see how Rob was doing, Mum would tell me how she'd been up all night praying that God would heal him. "I believe God can heal him," she would say. "Don't you believe that?" Yes, I too believed God could heal Rob. God can do anything. And over the years I've known of several verifiable situations where God's supernatural healing was obvious. In his sermon, however, Rob also carefully documented a slew of healing hoaxes that have permeated Christianity and embarrassed the church.[1]

While God can heal, it certainly does not mean that He will … and we best not assume His intent in any situation. As we sought balance and focus regarding this issue, Rob's own words spoke to us again through the audio recorded sermon. As you consider what he stated, you will see his sincere devotion to the Lord and his intense burden to challenge people to focus on Him and Him only:

> In many churches today, the focus is on our ailments, on our illnesses and on our sicknesses, and so on. But the problem is that when that is the focus … we are focusing on ourselves rather than focusing on the Lord Jesus Christ and rather than focusing on

1. For his documentation on the subject of false "faith" healers, Rob quoted extensively from the book *The Experience Trap* by Kel Willis (Burwood, N.S.W.: Christian Growth Ministries Pub., 1996).

what the Bible is actually saying and telling us. Now you see, I am not for a moment suggesting that the Lord can't heal or can't bring miraculous things in people's lives, I am not suggesting that for a moment. The miraculous sign that the Lord gives us (and the sign that we constantly need to be seeking and focusing on) is the sign where the Lord Jesus came into this world and gave up His life and shed His blood that you and I could be drawn to Christ. He rose from the dead. This is the greatest sign in the history of this world, and it will be the greatest sign until the Lord Jesus comes again. This is the great miracle: Christ came into the world to give His life.

Was Rob not healed physically because we lacked faith?

Faith is an indispensable element of the Christian life, important in all aspects of our belief and hope. Some have wrongly assumed, however, that healing is dependent on our level of faith; they claim that if we had enough faith, we would always be healed. But is that the case? It sure wasn't for the Apostle Paul. While a man of incredible faith, he recognized the humbling gift of illness in his own life — even though he prayed in faith for its removal:

> So to keep me from becoming conceited because of the surpassing greatness of the revelations, a thorn was given me in the flesh, a messenger of Satan to harass me, to keep me from becoming conceited (2 Corinthians 12:7).

Robert addressed Paul's situation in his sermon, referring also to the suffering of Job:

Job was afflicted, where the Lord allowed the devil
to afflict Job and there the Lord allowed the devil to
afflict Paul and whatever this thorn was, it was incredibly painful. The word "torment" comes from the
word "buffeted" and it means "a fist crushing bones."
It means this: Whatever Paul had, it was brutally
painful. I don't know what it was, whether it was his
eye, or whatever it be, it was incredibly painful. In 2
Corinthians 12:8, Paul stated, "Three times I pleaded
with the Lord about this, that it should leave me."
Three times he asked the Lord to take it away. But it
didn't happen. It didn't go, so the question you see
that I must ask, the question I have to ask the Apostle Paul is, "Paul, why didn't you have enough faith?
That must be the whole problem, Paul. You didn't
work up enough faith. You didn't believe enough,
that is your problem." So many people face exactly
that sort of aspect today; so many people. By the
way, I want you to notice that Paul does not bind the
devil; nowhere does he rebuke, nowhere does he cast
this out, nowhere!

When Robert said that "So many people face that sort of
aspect today," I wonder if he had any idea that he would
soon be one of those "so many people." While many people
gathered around us in this time of need, some cruelly sug-
gested that there was a lack of faith on Robert's part and our
part, and that that's why Robert had not been healed. Yet
again, we see many biblical examples where faithful people
were not healed. In 2 Timothy 4:20, for example, we read,

Erastus remained at Corinth, and I left Trophimus, who was ill, at Miletus. I'm sure Paul prayed for Trophimus, and no one is condemned here for a lack of faith causing this man's sickness. The same Paul through whom God at other times had miraculously healed the lame — even raised the dead — left Trophimus knowing that, under the sovereignty of God, his ministry would not in any way be thwarted.

However, Paul also recognized that sickness is a "normal" part of this life. In 2 Corinthians 1:8, Paul takes this point further as he says, *For we were so utterly burdened beyond our strength that we despaired of life itself.* Paul knew toward the end of his life that he would probably be martyred. Certainly, God could have stopped this, and no doubt Paul prayed concerning this matter, but he also recognized that in a world where *people loved the darkness rather than the light* (John 3:19), death was also a "normal" course of events.

Please understand that this does not mean that we shouldn't seek medical help or should just "resign" ourselves to death. This is a position Rob never took. This is certainly not to say that we shouldn't pray for physical healing either. James 5 commands us to do so. Rob acknowledged that God can bring healing and at times does so for His purposes. However, this is certainly not the normal course of events in today's world. The "normal" course of events, as Rob has clearly stated, is this:

> People suffer all sorts of trauma in their fallen state. Even if God heals someone physically, eventually they still will have to succumb to the effects of sin and the curse on their physical body.... The Bible

makes it clear, including through the actions of Christ Himself, that local, temporary efforts to alleviate the curse, such as healing of sicknesses, binding up wounds, and so on, are to be encouraged.

The normal effects of the curse will always be realized; that's what we are to expect. Sooner or later, through disease, decay, or disaster, the bodies we live in will die and perish. *For you are dust, and to dust you shall return* (Genesis 3:19). Even if someone were miraculously healed of some ailment, they will one day succumb to the events of the fall and by one means or another their body will eventually die.

My wife Mally in the graveyard where her parents' graves are located.

16

What Then Do We Do?

It's impossible to describe all that I experienced as I continued to listen to my brother's voice through the audio recording. His words were so distinct, his voice so confident, and his instruction so urgent. The irony was so amazing. Here he was, describing the reasons behind the very situation he was in, laying a foundation through Genesis to explain his condition. Then, as he moved into the application section of the sermon, it was as if he began to instruct me personally, advising me of specific ways I could respond as I navigated my way through the issues that his illness had caused us to face. Without in any way negating the fact that we pray for physical healing, Rob challenged his congregation (and us) this way:

> I suggest that when we are talking to somebody who is sick, that we need to restructure our terminology, that we might go to the person and say, "Brother, sister, I want you to know that we love you dearly. I want you to know we can see how much you are sick, and we are really praying to the Lord for you. We are just praying for you, really praying. And we want you to know how much we want to help you, and we want to come and help you. I'd like to pray with you. We are going to bring some meals for your family. We want to help you."

Since Rob recognized that sickness is a normal part of this life (even though we can ask God for healing), he exhorted us to encourage the sick person, telling them that we love them and are praying for them — prayers that include asking for the strength and comfort of those being most affected. He then encouraged practical acts of service that help the suffering person and those closest to them with the burdens they face during the tribulation.

This was a good reminder for me. I had flown to Australia specially to spend time with my mother and the family. This time of need presented unending opportunity to encourage them and share the weight that they were all carrying. Around me, family and friends were extending helping hands in all sorts of ways. Each word was a clear expression of love and care; each thoughtful act helped them with the physical demands of those days.

Sadly, many people (including many Christians) didn't know how to handle the situation. Personally, I think this was because they didn't have a full understanding (like Rob did) of the sin-cursed nature of this world, and how we should view life through God's "eyes." Without that foundation, they didn't know how to cope with a man of God like Rob being in such terrible physical condition. Robert's disease caused him to lose considerable self-awareness and depleted his ability to communicate. It took a lot of physical work to be around him ... but for those who didn't have a biblical worldview, it took a lot of mental work, too. Without a scriptural understanding of what was going on, people felt very awkward in his presence.

Without a big picture perspective, some avoided the situation altogether, while others gave in to false hopes or false fears. These were all things that didn't reflect the truth, the truth that what Robert was going through was actually "normal." And, everyone (unless the Lord returns before that time) will go through circumstances leading to death. That is "normal" in this abnormal world! *And just as it is appointed for man to die once, and after that comes judgment* (Hebrews 9:27).

As I continued to listen to Rob's sermon, my mind had found closure on so many issues. Objectively, I now had specific confirmation to the answers that I had found through the big picture. Rob, too, was convinced that sin was the answer to the question "How do you explain death and suffering in a world where an all-powerful, loving, and just God exists?" Rob's message had also addressed many other issues regarding healing and "fairness" — issues that we would continue to face in the closing weeks of his life. But the closure for me was more than just theological or philosophical; it was deeply personal. Hearing Rob's voice again and receiving the message that God had prepared years before for him to give to me began to set my soul at peace.

God's Word had answered the deepest questions we were facing on earth. What God had created was originally very good and had become deeply corrupted and contaminated by sin. God has graciously allowed us to continue to live ... sometimes even extending life through supernatural healing. But because of sin, we all face illness, disease, and a certain death; that's the new norm on this earth since the Fall.

But what happens after that? What are we to expect as we pass from this earth into eternity? God's Word, starting in Genesis, shows us that God has a plan for us beyond the grave as well.

17

Beyond the Grave

Yet you do not know what tomorrow will bring. What is your life? For you are a mist that appears for a little time and then vanishes. Instead you ought to say, "If the Lord wills, we will live and do this or that." As it is, you boast in your arrogance. All such boasting is evil. So whoever knows the right thing to do and fails to do it, for him it is sin (James 4:14–17).

Sometimes facing reality can be quite discouraging. It's disillusioning when we see that life is not what we thought it would be, not what we had hoped for or expected. Our circumstances change in an instant for many reasons — sickness, accident, etc. Inside, we all harbor an innate desire for Eden — a world of security, intimacy, and provision…. But such a world no longer exists. Yet within the context of the fallen world around us, we can look forward to a peace and joy that supersedes our sin-tainted circumstances.

In John 16:33, Christ Himself said:

"I have said these things to you, that in me you may have peace. In the world you will have tribulation. But take heart; I have overcome the world."

While the original creation was perfect, it has now been corrupted by sin and reels in confusion in a vacuum of truth. Thankfully, God has not left us alone in hopelessness.

Through Christ and the Cross, He has purchased and pre-pared a way back to life for those who are willing to receive it … and that's important. It is really important, for soon enough life as we know it will end and our actions will follow us into eternity.

Let's deal now with good news and bad news. First the bad news.

I know things have been a little heavy up to this point, so let me give you a few uplifting (yes, uplifting) excerpts from Scripture in Genesis 5:

> And Adam fathered Seth … then he died. And Seth fathered Enosh … then he died. And Enosh fathered Kenan … and then died. Kenan became the father of Mahalelel … and then died.

Isn't that an uplifting passage of Scripture? If you're not picking up on this, there is a pattern here! It goes like this: And he died … and he died … and he died. Sure, that might not seem very uplifting, but in the big picture of what God has done through Christ and the Cross, it can actually be great news.

I remember a man who once took a non-Christian friend to church and pulled the pastor aside and said, "Now I want you to give a positive evangelistic sermon for my friend." What did the pastor do? He preached on the genealogies in Genesis 5 — each one ending with the words "… and he died." This man thought, "oh no … oh no … this is not going to reach my non-Christian friend! I wanted a passage talking about Jesus dying on the Cross and offering forgive-ness and eternal life!" But do you know what? The man's friend came to Christ because the passage kept repeating "and he died ... and he died ... and he died."

The man listened and thought, "I am going to die!" The passage challenged him so much that he made a choice to get things right with God. (You never know how the Lord's going to use various passages, do you?!)

But I want you to think about this for a moment. If you took that passage, deleted some of the names and wrote in your parents' and grandparents' names, and then wrote in your name on the bottom line, that would be accurate, wouldn't it! Since Adam, death has been reality for every one of our ancestors and that's the future for each one of us, isn't it? What a reminder to each one of us. Prior to the Lord's return, we will live in a world where every human is going to die.

That understanding gives us a different perspective as we look at things like 9/11, when the World Trade Center towers in New York City were hit by terrorists. People told me, "Oh, I am glad I wasn't in the World Trade Center. I would have died." Well, do you know what my response was? "Don't worry, your turn will come!" I am in no way trying to take away from the horrible thing that happened that day, nor do I negate the grief countless people share over those who perished there. My point is only this: Both the Christian worldview and secular humanist worldview agree that even if you were thousands of miles away from New York that day, you will still die one day. We often look at others who die and think "I'm glad that's not me" — but it will be you one day.

It's important to get past the "why people die" question — and face the fact that death is a reality. While reporting on a natural disaster, I once heard a television reporter ask, "If there's a God of love, why would He let so many people and children die?" We've answered that question with a firm understanding of sin. Now we need to look past that issue to the extremely practical and vital question that must be asked: What will happen when I die?

Rather than facing the reality of the grave, however, many people still get caught up in philosophical questions that keep them one step away from having to deal with their own mortality. "Why would God let so many innocent people die?" I hear this question all the time. But again, let's be honest; how many "innocent" people are there in this world? Some people might appear to be innocent compared to other people, but how many people could say they are totally innocent before God? We are descendants of Adam, born "in Adam." All have sinned and fall short of the glory of God (Romans 3:23). Nothing good dwells in our flesh (Romans 7:18). We are all dead in trespasses and sin (Ephesians 2:1). Without Christ, *the heart is deceitful above all things and desperately sick* [wicked] (Jeremiah 17:9); *none is righteous, no not one* (Romans 3:10).

Honestly, there are no innocent people anywhere in the world. That's why all people will die. That's why we need to think beyond the grave. We need to think beyond this short existence on earth and think about eternity. Eternity is a long time! It's forever. Why do we get so caught up in this life when we need to focus on where we will spend eternity? When it comes to death, it's not really a matter of "why," and it's certainly not a matter of "if." What matters is that death is imminent ... and left to ourselves, we stand condemned before a holy God.

We need to be looking toward forever.

Our sin has placed us on a course away from God. If we continue in that direction on earth, we will continue in that direction after death — existing in eternal separation from God in a place He calls hell, where punishment and isolation will forever be the norm. There are plenty of people who reject that biblical fact. They often ask questions such as, "Why would a loving God sentence people to a horrible place like hell?" The question implies that it's God's fault. But it's not. When we correctly understand who we are as descendants of Adam, and contemplate the implications of the Fall, then we should understand that it's not God's fault at all. As I've stated before, it's our fault.

And as we study Scripture, we find God doesn't want us to be in hell, *not wishing that any should perish, but that all should reach repentance* (2 Peter 3:9).

C.S. Lewis wrote that those who are in hell will to be there, and would be worse off in God's holy presence as unrepentants.[1] We, in Adam, separated ourselves from God through our sin, effectively saying we didn't want Him. Remember, the temptation was that we would be like Him, that we would be our own god, choosing our own right from wrong according to what seems good to us. Sin is far more than just actions; it's an act of high treason against the Creator and Sustainer of all life. God is a righteous God, and thus had to judge sin — but in reality, we have

---

1. C.S. Lewis, *The Great Divorce* (New York: Simon & Schuster, 1996).

sentenced ourselves to hell (eternal separation from God) by our actions to be independent of Him.

You can see the impasse this has caused: As the God of love, our Lord desires for us to be united with Him forever … but as the God of justice, He must punish sin and rebellion. Romans 6:23 says *the wages of sin is death*, and Hebrews 9:22 says that *without shedding of blood there is no forgiveness.* Yes, it is our fault that we are destined for hell and can do nothing to save ourselves, but is it possible that God, in His merciful and timeless wisdom, created a way out for us?

Now we come to the good news — the really good news about the first sacrifice.

> *And the LORD God made for Adam and for his wife garments of skins and clothed them. Then the LORD God said, "Behold, the man has become like one of us in knowing good and evil. Now, lest he reach out his hand and take also of the tree of life and eat, and live forever" — therefore the LORD God sent him out from the garden of Eden to work the ground from which he was taken* (Genesis 3:21–23).

God is a righteous God. All His ways are perfect, so He had to judge sin with death. Banished from Eden where the tree of life grew, the descendants of Adam and Eve would forever know illness, suffering, and death. Prior to driving them from the Garden, however, God clothed them with garments of skin. (That's the origin of clothing by the way; the first covering of our guilt.) But it's even more than that.

Adam and Eve's sons, Cain and Abel, knew they had to bring a sacrifice to God … so we know that someone had shown them that there needed to be a sacrifice because of sin. I believe that the very first sacrifice — the first blood sacrifice as a covering for sin — takes place right there in Genesis 3:21, where God killed an animal (or animals), and then used the skin(s) to clothe Adam and Eve. It is the first recorded incident of *nephesh* death, the first killing of something with flesh and blood. God is the one who provided the animal(s); He is the one who performed the sacrifice … and He did it for the sinners He loved. He was setting up the sacrificial system. We learn more about that from when the Israelites sacrificed animals time and time again.

This first sacrifice was a picture of what was to come in Jesus Christ — a looking forward to the redemption that could be ours in Christ. It's what we would call a "proto-gospel" — a preview of Christ and what He was to do on the Cross when God Himself provided the perfect sacrifice for the sins of all.

We see in this first sacrifice a picture of God's covering for the sin of Adam and Eve and a prophetic image of what is to come. It's right there in Genesis 3:15 where God chastises the serpent (the devil) and tells him, *"I will put enmity between you and the woman, and between your offspring and her offspring; he shall bruise your head, and you shall bruise his heel."*

This proto-gospel and these prophecies were realized when God Himself stepped into human history to become a man so He could pay the price for our sins, which was death. Through His Resurrection, He proved He had victory over death, and now offers us the gift of salvation. *For the death he died he died to sin, once for all, but the life he lives he lives to God* (Romans 6:10).

> *For while we were still weak, at the right time Christ died for the ungodly. For one will scarcely die for a righteous person — though perhaps for a good person one would dare even to die — but God shows his love for us in that while we were still sinners, Christ died for us. Since, therefore, we have now been justified by his blood, much more shall we be saved by him from the wrath of God* (Romans 5:6–9).

> *Therefore, just as sin came into the world through one man, and death through sin, and so death spread to all men because all sinned.... But the free gift is not like the trespass. For if many died through one man's trespass, much more have the grace of God and the free gift by the grace of that one man Jesus Christ abounded for many* (Romans 5:12–15).

The whole of Romans 5 draws a vivid contrast between Adam and Christ, a powerful comparison between the one whose sin initiated death and the One whose death can bring us life.

This book has sought, like all publications associated with Answers in Genesis, to give glory and honor to God as Creator. We are convinced of the truth of the biblical record of the real origin and history of the world and mankind. Part of this real history is the bad news that the rebellion of the first man, Adam, against God's command brought death, suffering, disease, and separation from God into this world. We see the results all around us. All of Adam's descendants are sinful from fertilization (Psalm 51:5) and have entered into this rebellion of sin. We therefore cannot live with a

Holy God but are condemned to separation from God. The Bible says that all are therefore subject to *eternal destruction, away from the presence of the Lord and from the glory of his might* (2 Thessalonians 1:9).

But the good news is that God has done something about it. *For God so loved the world, that he gave his only Son, that whoever believes in him should not perish but have eternal life* (John 3:16).

Jesus Christ — though totally sinless — suffered on behalf of mankind, paying the penalty for mankind's sin — the penalty of death and separation from God.

As I covered before, Leviticus 17 tells us that the life of a creature is in its blood; so blood represents life and there has to be a shedding of life to pay the penalty of death. Hebrews 9:22 says, *Without the shedding of blood there is no forgiveness of sins.* Indeed, sacrifices have been made (as we've seen with the Israelites) since the first one in the Garden, but the blood of bulls and goats can't wash away human sin (Hebrews 10:4).

Because we are not connected to the animal kingdom, human blood had to be shed … and it had to be perfectly sinless blood in order to sufficiently pay the price of all sin. A sinner can't pay the penalty for sin.

That's why God did the unthinkable: the Creator Himself stepped into history to be one of us, to be our substitute on the Cross. We rebelled against our Holy God; we don't even deserve to exist. But God not only allows us to exist, He also provided a way for us to come back to be with Him. Through Christ's death on the Cross, He satisfied the righteous demands of the holiness and justice of God His

Father. Jesus was the perfect sacrifice; but on the third day He rose again, conquering death. All who truly believe in Him, repent of their sin, and trust in Him (rather than their own efforts), are able to come back to God and live now and for eternity with their Creator.

because, if you confess with your mouth that Jesus is Lord and believe in your heart that God raised him from the dead, you will be saved (Romans 10:9).

Whoever believes in him is not condemned, but whoever does not believe is condemned already, because he has not believed in the name of the only Son of God (John 3:18).

There is therefore now no condemnation for those who are in Christ Jesus. For the law of the Spirit of life has set you free in Christ Jesus from the law of sin and death (Romans 8:1–2).

Therefore, since we have been justified by faith, we have peace with God through our Lord Jesus Christ (Romans 5:1).

Those who receive this incredible gift of forgiveness and new life undergo a radical spiritual transformation ... one in which they are "born again" (John 3:3). While all people are descendants of Adam and were born "in Adam," those who give their lives to God and receive His payment and forgiveness for their sins are spiritually reborn "in Christ."

> *Therefore, if anyone is in Christ, he is a new creation. The old has passed away; behold, the new has come. All this is from God, who through Christ reconciled us to himself and gave us the ministry of reconciliation* (2 Corinthians 5:17–18).

> *I have been crucified with Christ. It is no longer I who live, but Christ who lives in me. And the life I now live in the flesh I live by faith in the Son of God, who loved me and gave himself for me* (Galatians 2:20).

What a wonderful Savior — and what a wonderful salvation in Christ our Creator! By receiving His free gift of new life you can begin the great adventure of renewing and reclaiming His original intent for humanity, one in which you walk with him and talk with him as His child. His inerrant Word lays the foundation of truth upon which this new life is constructed; its timeless principles and insights are *living and active* (Hebrews 4:12).

Struggles with the fallen world and sinful flesh will continue while on this earth, but beyond the grave, rather than eternal separation from Him forever, you will leave this world and your sinful body behind and enter into a perfect and pure relationship with Him in heaven forever.

Dear reader, if you have yet to come to Christ for forgiveness of sin and to have the assurance of eternal life with Him, do it now before it is too late. Nothing else offers any hope, and nothing else makes sense of all of reality. This is where the "big picture" must become your picture. You must receive His free gift of salvation. If you are having difficulty reconciling Bible/science issues, check out the Answers in Genesis website, www.AnswersInGenesis.org, where you'll find a wealth of information, resources, answers, and encouragement. If God has used this book to point you to the truth and you've become a believer, we would love for you to write and tell us; and of course, we would encourage you to commit to a strong Bible-believing church.

Let me be very straightforward with you right now. If you are rejecting God and Christ because of questions you have regarding suffering and death, it's time to get past that. As I've shown you, there are sound and reasonable answers from Scripture regarding these questions, but if you choose to dwell on these issues, basing your objections on what you (as a fallible finite human being) think is right and wrong, you're going to miss the point. The point right now isn't why death and suffering exist, or why some seem to suffer more or die sooner than others ... the point is that you will die, and you need to be prepared for that reality.

Christ faced these same objections in Luke 13. Someone brought up a supposed unjust situation where Pilate had killed Galilean citizens and mixed their blood with his sacrifices (a hideous atrocity for sure). Jesus cut to the real issue, however, with this response:

And he answered them, "Do you think that these Galileans were worse sinners than all the other Galileans, because they suffered in this way? No, I tell you; but unless you repent, you will all likewise perish. Or those eighteen on whom the tower in Siloam fell and killed them: do you think that they were worse offenders than all the others who lived in Jerusalem? No, I tell you; but unless you repent, you will all likewise perish" (Luke 13:2–5).

So when Jesus was asked why these people died, He basically answered by saying, "Repent." In other words, this was the time for these people to die, and you need to be looking at yourself and not them and asking yourself what will happen to you when you die.

Issues of "fairness" and supposed "injustice" may pester us for the rest of our lives, but the core issue that Jesus focuses on is the one we have already stated: They died. It was their time. You are going to die. Now is your time to repent and turn to the Lord. Make sure you have committed your life to Christ, for death is a reality, and what happens beyond the grave is determined on your decisions in life.

18

Beauty from Ashes

> *The Spirit of the Lord GOD is upon me, because the Lord has anointed me to bring good news to the poor; he has sent me to bind up the brokenhearted, to proclaim liberty to the captives, and the opening of the prison to those who are bound ... to comfort all who mourn ... to give them a beautiful headdress instead of ashes ...* (Isaiah 61:1–3).

In his book *Holy Sweat*,[1] Tim Hansel coined the phrase "turn your theology into your biography." That's an interesting concept, and by stating it Hansel implies that our theology (what we believe about God) doesn't normally match up with our biography (the actual course of our life). This mismatch can create a great gap between our expectations about what we think life should be like and our experiences in reality. In this gap can grow the roots of great disappointment — roots that grow into the question, "How do you explain death and suffering in a world where an all-powerful, loving, and just God exists?"

As we've stated earlier, the question is not just a smokescreen that unbelievers put up to avoid facing the gospel (though many do so quite frequently), it's a question believers wrestle with to a great extent as well. It's probably the

---

1. Tim Hansel, *Holy Sweat* (Dallas, TX: Word Publishing, 1987)

most agonized over question down through the ages by
Christians too. From our human perspective it just doesn't
seem resolvable because we just can't make sense of every
situation. But we are not God. We don't know everything.
Isn't it possible there are things we don't know that could
totally change our understanding of these circumstances?
But regardless of that, the point is, as we've discussed above,
God does answer the question, but just not every question
we might have about it.

For some reason, many Christians have picked up the
notion that everything should begin to work out the way
they want now that they have given their lives to Christ.
And when reality doesn't match expectations, disappointment and disillusionment are the result. Theologically, we
know who God is, and we know that He is good. But when
we look at our biography, we see a trail of pain and suffering
(not exactly the way we would expect a loving Father to treat
His children). So, philosophically speaking, the problem of
evil turns out to be a problem for the believer as well.

Desperately we seek reconciliation between the pain and
evil we experience and this loving God we believe in. We
can now clearly see that sin is the root cause of suffering
and death, but somehow, this evil has to be compatible with
God's goodness. And that's where we struggle big time.

God created everything, knows everything, is all powerful, and exists in all places. He is also the embodiment and
definer of "good." Somehow, our theology and our biography must be meshed on this point. Some people (like Turner
and Darwin) change their theology in the face of difficult
events and turn against God. But since God is unchanging

(Malachi 3:6), and the inerrant Word of God clearly tells us who He is, the only thing we can rightly change is our attitude and our perspective toward evil, and trust what God has revealed to us in His Word. We can't just reason autonomously on this, or any, issue. We can reason, but not without faith and trust in His Word.

With that in mind, I'd like to turn to a well-known and well-worn passage of God's Word, Romans 8:28:

> *And we know that for those who love God all things work together for good, for those who are called according to his purpose.*

I bring up this portion of the Bible with some hesitancy. Too often it has been used as a superficial band-aid, slapped on gaping wounds as a quick fix for deeply rooted pain and difficulty. These words are not some cure-all cliché to be thrown at someone who is hurting. This is the Word of God … something to be seriously considered and applied, recognized for what it says and for what it does not say.

First, it's important to notice that the verse does not say that all things are good. Paul is clearly acknowledging in this passage (as he does in many, many others) that bad things exist, and bad things happen. The passage simply says that *all things work together for good*. Secondly, this passage is reserved for those *who love God* and *are called according to his purpose*. This passage does not apply to those who have rejected God and are continuing to live in independence from Him. An entirely different fate awaits them. So, what this passage does say is that God causes all things — even evil events — to occur for reasons that are morally commendable and good.

> *I form light and create darkness; I make well-being and create calamity; I am the LORD, who does all these things* (Isaiah 45:7).

Apologist G.L. Bahnsen said this:

> If the Christian presupposes that God is perfectly and completely good — as Scripture requires us to do — then he is committed to evaluating everything within his experience in the light of that presupposition. Accordingly, when the Christian observes evil events or the things in the world, he can, and should, retain consistency with his presupposition about God's goodness by now inferring that God has a morally good reason for the evil that exists. God certainly must be all powerful in order to be God; He is not to be thought of as overwhelmed or stymied by evil in the universe. And God is surely good, the Christian will profess — so any evil we find must be compatible with God's goodness. This is just to say that God has planned evil events for reasons which are morally commendable and good.[2]

Theoretically, that's not too difficult to understand. Practically, however, it's often very tough to accept. When we stare evil events in the face — feeling their full weight and implications — it's difficult to believe Romans 8:28. Thankfully, we don't have to rely solely on our own biography to

---

2. G.L. Bahnsen, *Always Ready — Directions for Defending the Faith* (Nacogdoches, TX: Covenant Media Press, 2002), p. 171–172.

see that this verse is true. Numerous examples from the Bible illustrate that evil events have been planned by God to work for the good.

The account of Esther is a powerful example of God's omniscient plan that causes all things to work for good. The event takes place in the days of King Ahasuerus, who reigned from India to Ethiopia. The king was searching far and wide for a new wife to be his queen, and that's when he discovered Esther.

> *Now there was a Jew in Susa the citadel whose name was Mordecai … who had been carried away from Jerusalem among the captives carried away with Jeconiah king of Judah, whom Nebuchadnezzar king of Babylon had carried away. He was bringing up Hadassah, that is Esther, the daughter of his uncle, for she had neither father nor mother. The young woman had a beautiful figure and was lovely to look at, and when her father and her mother died, Mordecai took her as his own daughter* (Esther 2:5–7).

The king was initially unaware that Esther was a Jewess. But after a huge selection process, he chose her as his queen. Sometime after Esther had become queen, a wicked man named Haman plotted to have all Jews killed. Because Esther had access to the king, she alone was in the position to petition the king to save the Jews. But according to the laws of the land, if Esther approached the king on this matter, she would likely be killed.

When Mordecai (Esther's uncle who had looked after her) sent a message to Esther, urging her to petition the king, she sent him this reply:

> *"All the king's servants and the people of the king's provinces know that if any man or woman goes to the king inside the inner court without being called, there is but one law — to be put to death, except the one to whom the king holds out the golden scepter so that he may live. But as for me, I have not been called to come in to the king these thirty days"* (Esther 4:11).

You can imagine the tension as Esther struggled with what she should do. Still, Mordecai saw beyond the initial threat. He saw not only the urgency of the situation, but he also saw God's hand in placing Esther where she was ... and he exhorted her with these words:

> *Then Mordecai told them to reply to Esther, "Do not think to yourself that in the king's palace you will escape any more than all the other Jews. For if you keep silent at this time, relief and deliverance will rise for the Jews from another place, but you and your father's house will perish.* **And who knows whether you have not come to the kingdom for such a time as this?"** (Esther 4:13–14, emphasis added).

Mordecai not only realized the powerful position Esther was in, but also challenged Esther to think in terms of God's sovereign plan for her life. Could it be that all the circumstances of the past — circumstances that had resulted in her being queen — were planned by God just for this vital occasion?

I'm sure Esther thought about her childhood and all that had happened to her. Then she stepped out in faith to save her people.

During that time, the king also read a record of Mordecai's past actions revealing that Mordecai had saved the king from an evil conspiracy. These events became entwined in a fascinating and twisted series of circumstances that revealed the plot in which Haman had attempted to manipulate the king to eliminate the Jewish people. When the king realized the truth, Haman ended up being sentenced to death.

I've often wondered what was going through Mordecai's mind after the Jews were saved. I'm sure he pondered the past events surrounding his niece Esther — the events that so long ago had brought them together "for such a time as this." Perhaps he and Esther understood that it was the death of Esther's parents that ultimately led to the saving of an entire nation. The details of Esther's parents have been lost from history. Were her parents killed? Did they die at an early age from some horrible disease? We do not know. Did people look at Esther and say, "Why would God allow this beautiful little young girl to lose her parents and why would that happen?" And yet, as we now stand back and see her place in the big picture, you can see the morally commendable reasons that God had. Through the tragic death of her parents, God brought Esther into the home of Mordecai in circumstances that led to the saving of an entire group of people.

Think about it — who would have guessed that God would use an arrogant pagan king and a queen who wouldn't obey him, an evil man who set out to kill the Jews, a young

girl who lost her parents, and a godly man called Mordecai to save the Jewish people? And the fascinating thing is
God's name is not even mentioned in the Book of Esther,
but we see His hand in all these events for a special purpose. What an example to us that, even though at the time
we can't see why God would allow such circumstances, we
know He is working in ways we couldn't have imagined.
Sometimes we can look back and see God's hand in circumstances (as we can look back at what happened with
Esther) and marvel at what God did. Other times we don't
seem to be able to see why things happened, and maybe we
won't even find out till we are in heaven.

In addition to this fascinating event, Esther's life and
actions were recorded and made a part of the Holy Word
of God for all eternity. How many millions and millions of
times has the Book of Esther been read, changing hearts and
lives? At the time of her parent's death, I doubt that anyone
would have imagined that God would "cause" those tragic
circumstances to "work together for good." From a human
perspective, it would have only seemed to be grossly unfair.

A similar situation exists with my dad and the death of
his father. There's no doubt that my father had an unusual
love for the Bible. Years after his death, I still remember
when I used to walk into the house and see him sitting in his
favorite chair with his reading glasses on, a pen in his hand,
and his copiously marked Bible in his lap.

Dad was a teacher, and, as a public school principal,
was transferred to many different towns around the State of
Queensland. Dad and Mum started Sunday schools and/
or ran Bible studies everywhere they went. They hosted

missionaries and sponsored outreach programs to reach children and adults. In fact, it was at one of these programs in Innisfail, North Queensland, that I went forward at a meeting to make a commitment to be a missionary for the Lord.

Dad and Mum with their first two children, myself and sister Rosemary.

Dad hated it when the Bible was knowingly compromised and would always stand up for what he believed, regardless of the persecution he would receive. One Sunday, for example, we were in church, and the pastor preached about the boy who provided the five thousand with the few loaves and fishes. The pastor said that what happened wasn't really a miracle, but that because a little boy took out his loaves and fishes, he set a great example for the others to follow, and they then took out their own food and shared it with each other. My father was very upset! At the end of the service, he led the whole family up to the pastor and began challenging him from the Bible, proving conclusively that this was, indeed, a miracle. He would preface his statements with "It is written ..." as he expounded on the Bible's account of this event.

Many years later, as Dad lay dying in a hospital, Robert asked him, "Dad, why did you have such a love for the Word of God? What was it that caused you to stand so strongly on Scripture?" I had never asked Dad about this, and my heart raced — I couldn't wait to hear the answer. Dad told Rob that when he was only 16 years old, his father died. It was a great personal loss to a young lad. But because he no longer had an earthly father to turn to, he turned to his Heavenly Father, reading His Word over and over again, becoming more and more committed to its message and more and more convinced of its authority. As I listened to Rob, I became rather choked up. Yes, it made sense. Dad seemed to be always reading the Bible — he really loved God's Word, and that love emerged out of tragic circumstances. This love overflowed into our family, influencing our entire upbringing.

My dad's passion for the Bible is one of the major reasons Rob had such a love for the Word of God and worked so hard to tell others about the gospel. (Rob was also a "chip off the old block," as people say.) He was like Dad in so many ways, never compromising the Scriptures, always standing up for what he believed was right, regardless of the consequences. And there's no doubt in my mind that I would not have founded Answers in Genesis, the Creation Museum and Ark Encounter (outreaches that now reach tens of millions of

My favorite photo of Dad teaching God's Word at a Bible study.

people each year) if it weren't for my father and mother's stand on the Word of God.

Who would have thought that when my Dad was a teenager, his father's death would be used by God to lead to millions of people hearing about God's infallible, authoritative Word and the saving gospel?

I've recalled these events in my mind many times over the years, particularly as I've thought about what happened to Rob. As I pondered these things in my heart, something became very clear to me — something that has been of great comfort in the midst of terrible sorrow: God does cause all things to work

My father with his Bible (that is now in the Ham Family Legacy Exhibit at the Creation Museum) and mother off to church.

My father on holidays in front of their Caravan studying God's Word.

together for good even if we can't see it at the time, and even if we can't see it later either.

The death of Esther's parents and the death of my grandfather are only two examples of God using suffering, division, and death to work for a greater good. In Acts 15:39–41, we see how God used a bitter disagreement between Paul and Barnabas to cause a split in their ministries — a division which resulted in both Cyprus and Syria being reached with the gospel. Similarly, persecution faced by the Antioch church was used to disperse them throughout the surrounding region, preaching about Christ as they went (Acts 14:5–7). The account of Joseph, of course, is a classic example of God using the sinful intent of his brothers for great good. Read this amazing account for yourself in Genesis 39–50.

The only photo I have of Dad's father (left) then his sister and mother and Dad at back.

You'll see the unmistakable hand of God leading Joseph into great injustices in order to bring him to a position where he saved countless lives from starvation. When he faced the brothers who had caused him such strife, Joseph comforted them with these words:

> But Joseph said to them, "Do not fear, for am I in the place of God? As for you, you meant evil against me, but God meant it for good, to bring it about that many people should be kept alive, as they are today. So do not fear; I will provide for you and your little ones." Thus he comforted them and spoke kindly to them (Genesis 50:19–21).

By anyone's standards, Joseph endured great hardship and betrayal (in spite of the fact that he continually chose to live uprightly in all situations). Looking back, it's clear to see that God had planned the evil against him for morally commendable and good reasons.

Sometimes the good that comes out of suffering is quite incidental to the circumstances, proving that God shows infinite creativity in causing all things to work for good. Think about the suffering of Job. While Job was dealing with the onslaught of suffering and loss in his life, I'm sure that the last thing he was thinking about was the possibility that a book (inspired by God) would one day be written outlining all the details of what happened to him ... a book that was to be incorporated into the holy written Word of God, used to teach generation after generation necessary truths that God wanted us to understand.

I often quote the Book of Job in my talks on Genesis. In Job 40:15, while using creation as proof of His power and control, God describes an animal and that description can certainly fit that of a sauropod dinosaur. We don't know for sure what the animal was, but it's certainly possible it could be a dinosaur. Thousands of children and adults have benefited from this teaching as an important piece in the big picture of history. And my close friend Buddy Davis wrote a song about this creature, titled *Behemoth Is a Dinosaur*, that thousands of children (and adults) have enjoyed singing.

One of my favorite verses of the Bible is also found in Job 38:4, *"Where were you when I laid the foundation of the earth? Tell me, if you have understanding."* God rebuked Job with this question when he questioned God's role in the ill that had befallen him. I teach children and adults all over the world to ask the same question (respectfully) to secularists who claim that life has evolved over millions of years: "Were you there?" I have heard so many testimonies from parents who say this has helped their children combat the false teaching regarding origins and the age of the earth. As a result of Job, many children have asked evolutionary scientists, "Were you there?" (And if the scientist replies, "No — but you weren't either," I have taught the children to respond, "No, I wasn't there but I know someone who was, and I have His Word. Are you interested?")

19

The Vantage Point of Time

We can't see things from an eternal perspective. Only God can. Only God can foresee all the events and orchestrate plans beyond our comprehension. He is God! We need to ponder that every day! We are not told of the events surrounding the death of Esther's parents. Perhaps they died of some horrible disease or were tragically killed by the invading army that forced the Israelites into exile. At the time of their death, some Jews might have questioned why God would allow a young girl to lose both her parents. Maybe even Mordecai questioned in his heart why God would allow such a seemingly terrible situation to befall such a lovely young girl as Esther. At the time of the tragedy, no human being could foresee the future; yet God was working out a plan beyond what anyone could have imagined. Esther was being placed in circumstances such that she would be used by God to save the Jewish people ... but no one could see it at the time.

When I look back at the history of Answers in Genesis, the Creation Museum and Ark Encounter, I can now see God's hand in circumstances that at the time I didn't understand. There were events that caused me to cry out to the Lord saying something like, "Lord, it's not fair. It's not right. Why should they be allowed to get away with this?" At one time, there were some circumstances that seemed destructive to the ministry, and I had to come to the point of recognizing that AiG is God's ministry, not mine. He has a right to do with it what He wants. And now we look back and see God did amazing things to direct us in ways we could never have thought of. Yes, after over 40-plus years in ministry, I've seen evil events occur from within and without. Although I don't understand them all, I can see how God used them to expand the ministry and reach millions more than we ever envisioned. And He has used such events to also save the ministry from people who would have eventually destroyed it. God knows all, He knows our hearts, and He orchestrates everything for His purposes.

When my father's father died, those close to the situation grieved greatly. Some may have even commented that it didn't seem fair that a young lad like my dad would be left on this earth without his father. Some might even have been angry at God, or perhaps some might have mocked Christians who believed in a holy, loving, and just God in the midst of such a situation.

However, many years later, we can look back and see the good that God worked — good that no one would have even come close to guessing at the time. The situation that caused my father to turn to his Heavenly Father (and ultimately igniting his passion for the Bible) resulted in a godly family who stood on the authority of the Word of God. Rob became a preacher of the Word. I was instrumental in founding a ministry that has grown around the world. Others in the family have been involved in various Christian ministries. All of this put new meaning into the verse of Scripture many often quote when tragedy strikes, *"For my thoughts are*

*not your thoughts, neither are your ways my ways, declares the
LORD"* (Isaiah 55:8).

The worship song "In His Time" puts these truths to
music with these words:

> In His time, in His time
> He makes all things beautiful
> In His time.
> Lord, please show me every day
> As You're teaching me Your way
> That You do just what You say
> In Your time.

Nowhere is this timing more evident than in the events surrounding the death and Resurrection of Jesus Christ. Without question, His brutal death on the Cross was the most
unjust evil event in the history of all humanity ... an absolutely sinless and perfect man beaten to a pulp, hung with
spikes through His own flesh, left gasping in the hot sun
while the jeers of the mocking crowd filled the air.

Those closest to Him hid in fear and disillusionment.
The hopes of the masses (who thought Him to be the chosen
Savior) were buried with His broken and bloody body, sealed
in despair as the rock was rolled across the opening of the
tomb. From anyone's perspective it was a horrible, devastating event — but time would prove differently.

Just three days later the unthinkable — the unimaginable
— had happened. The tomb was empty, and rumors circu-
lated of the impossible: He was alive! The sunrise that Sunday
morning revealed that the Son had risen. As the reality of
the news was confirmed by His appearances, the whole of

human history was altered forever.

Still in shock over their loss, the followers of Christ realized that the most evil of deaths had resulted in the greatest victory conceivable: the perfect sacrifice had been given for sin. Victory over the grave was now a possibility. A new covenant of grace and freedom replaced the bondage of legalism and slavery to religion. The price of redemption had been paid, sealing the promise of forgiveness and opening the door to an intimate relationship with the Creator once again. God had caused horrible circumstances to work together for good, and as a result the most evil of events was transformed into the most glorious of realities.

From the perspective of time and the Resurrection, we can even see death itself as a moral good. Death is properly called the "last enemy" (1 Corinthians 15:26). But in a strange and obvious way, it is also a blessing for mankind. Ultimately, without death, humanity would have no way of experiencing complete reconciliation with God. Confined in

our bodies of sinful flesh, our separation from Him would be eternal, but for those who believe in Christ, death is the doorway into a glorious future.

Romans 8:28 is far from cliché. Those who are willing to consider the deeper implications of this truth, looking to examples in the Bible for support, will find the hope and faith to carry on in the midst of suffering and death. That has certainly been the case for me ... even with my brother Robert. The circumstance behind his illness and the loss caused by his death sent shock waves through my soul. But I believe that we will see God work this for good, both now and from the perspective of eternity.

In many ways, I can see it already. Rob's story has been read by many thousands in a previous book entitled, *How Could a Loving God?* Hundreds of thousands have been touched by his example as I have spoken around the world. Many people have written to me to tell me that they have read many books on death and suffering ... but they say that Robert's story has helped them because it is "real life" — down-to-earth reality — that is dealt with head-on with the Bible, starting in the Book of Genesis. And as I speak and write on this topic, I believe it's important to admit my own struggles, regardless of how strong my Christian faith is. And we all have those struggles. We all ask the "why" questions — and that's okay. We're human.

Already I realize that my brother Robert has ministered more to people in his death than he did in his life. Lord willing, many thousands more will read this greatly expanded and updated book as well, finding answers, hope, and eternal salvation. Was his death "untimely" and "terrible"? Most certainly. But the God who is in the business of taking evil and using it for good has orchestrated it for reasons that are clearly morally commendable.

Even though it doesn't stop the grief — and I must admit I still heave a sigh and shake my head in disbelief — it has been a great comfort to be reminded that God is still working through the circumstances surrounding Rob's illness and death. Maybe something even greater than Esther's situation could come out of this — who knows?

God's Word is clear, and examples from the Bible and contemporary life are plentiful. With a little faith we can begin to see good in many of the circumstances we face in this fallen world … and that faith gives hope and perspective.

Though it is often difficult to see the good while the bad events are happening, it doesn't take too much imagination to see the potential for good in all that happens, particularly when we look not just at the outward circumstances, but when we focus on how God uses the outward struggles to conform us to Christ on the inside. Almost always, the good He is causing becomes more evident when we are willing to wait so we can look back from the vantage point of time.

Another passage of Scripture that has helped me come to grips with this issue from the vantage of time is 2 Peter 3:8–9. In response to the scoffers who questioned the promise that Jesus is coming back because the "last days" just seem to go on and on (and have done so for 2,000 years since Jesus promised to return), Peter states:

But do not overlook this one fact, beloved, that with the Lord one day is as a thousand years, and a thousand years as one day. The Lord is not slow to fulfill his promise as some count slowness, but is patient toward you, not wishing that any should perish, but that all should reach repentance.

Now this passage has nothing to do with defining the word "day" in the context of the days of creation as some people falsely claim. It is teaching us that to God, a day is like a thousand years, or a thousand years is like a day. In other words, God is not limited by natural processes and time. God is outside of time. He exists in eternity. To us, events might seem to happen so slowly, but not to God. Many times in the Old Testament we read prophecies that were fulfilled hundreds or even thousands of years later. We read how God allowed pagan kings to invade Israel and do wicked things and seem to get away with it. But in time, God uses others to judge them for their wickedness, even though God used them at the time to judge His people for their rebellion. God does things in His time, for His purposes. We have to come to grips with that.

I've sometimes said to people about so many of the evil politicians we see in Washington DC, "If we were God, there would be charred bodies all over DC." In other words, I don't understand why God is not judging these evil people who want to kill children in the womb and destroy children through sexualization, gender ideology, and other evil beliefs. But they will answer to God one day. And maybe God is using them as judgment on a nation where so many have turned away from Him. Who knows how God is using all this for His own purposes and to save people? Remember what Joseph said about how all the evil that happened to him was so that many would be kept alive? And even though we despair at what we see happening in our Western nations concerning morality and the increasing attacks on Christianity, God is in control. We need to be faithful and trust Him and obey Him. And regardless of what happens, we do need to be doing the business of the King until He returns. And that "business" is proclaiming the truth of God's Word and the saving gospel. The parable Jesus told in Luke 19 is to teach us to use whatever resources/talents God has entrusted us and *"engage in business until I come"* (Luke 19:13).

Actually, the Christian freedoms we have enjoyed in the West for a long time have really been abnormal. What we see happening now is more "normal" in a fallen world where there's more on the broad way than the narrow one. Remember that when we hear people asking, "Where is God?" when we see such evil leaders and moral relativism permeating the culture. This is more "normal" in this abnormal world.

In most situations (but certainly not all), when we look at evil with the big picture in mind, God's working for good will be visible — even when we can only glimpse small slivers of His light in the midst of the darkness. But what are we to do when we can't see the good at all? In those times we must bend the knee before our sovereign God, trusting that from the perspective of eternity His goodness in the midst of the evil will be revealed.

20

Bowing the Knee

In the course of the Christian life, seasons emerge that push the boundaries of our belief in the goodness of God, causing doubt about His willingness and/or ability to truly "work all things for good." War, famine, the loss of a loved one, financial concerns, divorce, a wayward child, bankruptcy, physical disability, painful disease … anything that threatens the things that we feel are essential to a meaningful life expose the vulnerability of human faith.

Situations that appear to be terminal — those with no hope of healing or reconciliation — hit home the hardest. Though our lives may be filled with belief and conviction in God, in each of our hearts there comes a point where "the good" cannot be imagined; in every soul there are boundaries to faith … and certain circumstances can push us beyond those limits into a place where doubt and despair rule.

King David, the writer of the majority of the Psalms, was no stranger to this place. His words regularly describe hopelessness, depression, and — perhaps worst of all — the sense that God had abandoned him. Consider, for example, Psalm 44:23–25:

> *Awake! Why are you sleeping, O Lord? Rouse yourself!*
> *Do not reject us forever! Why do you hide your face? Why*
> *do you forget our affliction and oppression? For our soul*
> *is bowed down to the dust; our belly clings to the ground.*

The situations that strike at our souls the most powerfully are usually the ones that are closest to our hearts: the issues of "life" that challenge our core beliefs about what is "right," the dreams that we don't even know we have, the expectations that lie central to our hopes, the tragedies that reveal our true beliefs about what should be. When circumstances press against these issues, our faith (as tattered as it may be at the moment) becomes vital for spiritual survival.

During the last days that I had with my brother, I held his hand tightly, but my faith clung desperately to God. "Lord," I said quietly, "I don't understand. He wants to tell them about You — why can't he do that? Why have You let this happen to him? It just doesn't make sense to me." As I despairingly looked at Rob, my mind traced the circumstances that had brought him to this place. It seemed like such an inappropriate end, so contrary to where we thought life would take him. It all appeared to be a total loss compared to how we thought God would use him.

As I sat at his side, my mind flashed back to the days when Robert was a successful bank manager. Through his upright character and dedicated work, he was "climbing the ladder of success" rather quickly. He had a great future in this financial institution, already enjoying a secure job with an excellent salary and many other benefits. But deep inside, Rob was wrestling with his real passion … a passion to preach. Just like our father, he loved the Word of God. It greatly distressed him to see preachers who did not believe the Bible regularly compromising its content and authority. Rob was deeply involved in his local church and he began lay preaching. In preparation, he read and reread sermons by some of the greats like Martyn Lloyd-Jones and Charles Haddon Spurgeon ... and all the while his desire to be in full-time ministry grew.

During that time, my wife and I went full time into the creation apologetics ministry now known as Answers in Genesis. Rob's family often gave us much-needed financial support. In those days the ministry was very small, and finances were rather scarce. Rob's financial support helped us more than he realized, providing for our most basic needs through those financially trying years.

As the burden on Rob to preach increased, he believed God had definitely called him to leave the bank and go to a theological college so he could study God's Word and become a teacher of the Bible. He and his family sacrificed much so he could earn this theological degree. They moved to Sydney, a very expensive place to live in Australia. To keep expenses down, they rented a house that was part of a chicken farm on the outskirts of this great city. The first time I visited, I was somewhat shocked at the horrible smell from thousands and thousands of chickens. I'm not sure I could have put up with it. Rob spent many hours a day commuting by train, bus, or car. Every possible moment during the commute was spent studying and preparing sermons.

Soon, the money saved from his years at the bank was gone, but my wife and I were now in a position to support Rob and his family financially, just as they had done for us.

Rob studied hard ... a seemingly unending string of long days and short nights. But he was a good student, and his reputation was growing as an effective communicator of the Word of God. When his formal education was finally complete, we gave Rob a complete set of Spurgeon's works as a graduation present.

Our regular phone conversations now focused on what his next step should be. He wanted to find a church where he could reach out to the community. He also had a burden to reach Muslims and students for Christ. Underneath it all was his intense burden to preach the gospel of Christ. The bottom line was that he just wanted to reach everyone he could with the message of salvation.

After considering several offers, he was led to take up a position as pastor in a church on Australia's Gold Coast. Australia has a very small percentage of Christians and is a very pagan country. I still remember the day he invited me along as he visited with the head deacon of this church. Rob was excited, really excited. His passion was developing into a specific vision for his ministry. Not far from the church was a major university and he saw great potential for reaching the students there. The church was in a community desperately in need of the gospel. As his vision clarified, he saw how this small church in the middle of it all could be used by God to make a difference.

Once he was at the church, Rob threw his heart and soul into his ministry. He continued to study hard. He taught the Word of God verse-by-verse and applied it practically in today's world. Rob also had a special gift for playing the piano. After playing for the hymns and choruses, he would then get up and teach the Word of God. The church began to grow. Some people who visited the Gold Coast for holidays heard that they could hear the Word of God taught uncompromisingly at Rob's church, so they would come and bring others. One of the most-asked questions I receive when I speak at the Ark Encounter or the Creation Museum is if I know of a church in a particular town that stands on God's Word as we do at Answers in Genesis. People tell me how hard it is to find such a church. And that is certainly true in Australia, and was the situation when Rob was a pastor.

Rob's church also hosted the American tourists that my wife and I brought over each year for a special tour of Australia. Rob would have me preach, and the church would provide lunch for the tourists. What great memories.

But it all began to fall apart just when Rob's ministry was having great effect ... after all the sacrifice and "blood, sweat, and tears," when he was beginning to fulfill the vision and burden he had for years ... and just as things seemed to be blessed and moving ahead. It was hard on all of us, but it was particularly hard on my mother — his mother. The terminal diagnosis, watching his mind and body decay before her eyes, preparing for the funeral.... I think what she went through can only be understood by others who have had to bury a child, and the situation stretched her faith beyond the point where she could even begin to imagine any good that might come out of this. "I know God is in control. I know this is a sin-cursed world. I understand all that. But I still don't understand why this would happen to him," she would cry out. "It doesn't seem to make sense! He worked so hard and preached so well. Why?" To a degree I still ask that question today.

During one of my many phone calls with Mum, she said in her grief, "It doesn't seem fair. He was such a man of God who loved and preached God's Word. There are all these people who compromise the Bible, and atheists who attack it. Why did this happen to such a person as Robert?"

We were all in the here-and-now, grieving over a situation that was hard to explain in the context of a loving God as described in the Bible. If Rob had been killed in a traffic accident or contracted some deadly disease like cancer, it would have been a terrible shock, and many would have grieved greatly (and we all would have probably asked many of the same questions), but somehow, this disease seemed particularly cruel. The very gift of communication the Lord had given to him was taken away, and it was as if he was then put on the rack to be slowly tortured to death while family and friends were (if possible) tortured even more. All we could do was watch as helpless spectators, groping for answers.

As family and friends, we wrestled hard with the questions. Why would God allow this? Why did he cause it? It just didn't seem right from our perspective. There are some people who will try to put you on a guilt trip if you ask those kinds of questions, insinuating that you don't have faith in God. We had faith, for certain, but it was being seriously tested. We're humans, and I believe we can ask those questions. We did as a family, and I did as a brother — I admit it. In the hardest moments of those dark days we all had to learn to stand back and say, "God is God," and then stand aside and let Him be God. And actually, that is not easy under such circumstances.

But for Mum it seemed much worse than that; this was her son. In the regular order of things, it should have been him comforting her as she lay on the threshold of death, not the other way around. Added to this was the fact that he was

My wife Mally and I with my mother in Australia.

leaving behind a young family. So not only did Mum struggle as a mother, but she struggled as a grandmother as well.

One time her frustration overflowed, and she said, "I don't understand it. The liberal pastor down the street who teaches against the Bible as the inerrant Word of God is as healthy as an ox. And look at my son who stood on the authority of the Word of God and he is suffering a horrible brain disease!" I said, "But Mum, you have got to remember something: What's happened to Robert is going to happen to the liberal pastor. He is going to die." I even shared with her what I was learning from the tape of Robert's sermon. I said "Mum, Robert himself said that death, suffering, and disease are normal in an abnormal world, and we live in an abnormal world because of sin."

I went over all the Bible verses with Mum about the sovereignty of God and about the Jesus of the Bible being in control. We looked at Romans 8:28 and how all things work together for good, and that God's ways are higher than ours, and so on. But she knew all that. It wasn't that her mind didn't understand, it just seemed that her heart could not withstand it. Yes, it was difficult for those of us who called him brother, husband, and father: but our circumstances were even more ominous for the one who called him son. Her own body had harbored Robert's tiny growing form. She was the one who held him to her breast as he took his first breaths, but now she was holding him again in her arms as he breathed his last.

What is one to do in such times when faith is stretched thin, and circumstances bear down hard? In such times there is no other choice but to bow the knee before God and place the remaining trust that He gives back at His feet.

During the toughest of times, we must fall back on a simple and powerful truth: God is God; we are not. God is the One (the only One) who determines what is right and what will be or not be. Our place is one of submission and obedience — regardless of the pain, regardless of the confusion. And we're told, *Your eyes saw my unformed substance; in your book were written, every one of them, the days that were formed for me, when as yet there was none of them* (Psalm 139:16). God is in total control of all that happens in our life, from when we were formed in our mother's womb to death. And as Ecclesiastes 3:2 puts it, there is *a time to be born, and a time to die.*

The Book of Isaiah deals with these issues and God's Sovereignty in all things extensively:

> *that people may know, from the rising of the sun and from the west, that there is none besides me; I am the LORD, and there is no other. I form light and create darkness; I make well-being and create calamity; I am the LORD, who does all these things* (Isaiah 45:6–7).

> *"Woe to him who strives with him who formed him, a pot among earthen pots! Does the clay say to him who forms it, 'What are you making?' or 'Your work has no handles'? Woe to him who says to a father, 'What are you begetting?' or to a woman, 'With what are you in labor?'"* (Isaiah 45:9–10)

When the dark times come, God offers no apologies and gives few explanations — and He takes responsibility for all that is taking place. *I am the Lord who does all these things.* Pour out your heart, if you wish, but don't argue. He is God, you are not. Period. None of us understand what He is doing and what will come of it. *Oh, the depth of the riches and wisdom and knowledge of God! How unsearchable are his judgments and how inscrutable his ways!* (Romans 11:33). Yes, God is the one who raises up kingdoms and destroys them. He's in charge of those sorts of things. He is a sovereign God and so nothing happens that He doesn't know about. As one of my friends said, "God has yet to make His first mistake and God is in total control." That's not a cop-out; that's simply allowing God to be God. Make no mistake on this point. God is very firm. He is who He is, and He has absolutely no obligation to us to change anything according to our desires, nor should He be compelled to alter His plans to pander to our feelings.

God is God; we are not. Because of that, we have little choice but to pour out our hearts to Him in full honesty and then make a definitive decision to recognize God for who He is. Then we must humbly bow before Him and His purposes in faith.

David repeats this same pattern many times in the Psalms: an honest outpouring of his heart … followed by recognition of God's character … followed by a decision to submit and worship in the midst of suffering, danger, and death. This is the pattern we see in the Book of Job as well.

Everything that Job cares about is taken from him — everything, including his children. In its place he is stricken with suffering and physical agony. His friends gather round to figure out his problem. (None of them got it right, by the way. They never did find out what was happening behind the scenes … and they would have been of much more help had they kept their mouths shut and tried to serve Job in some tangible way.) The conversation between Job and his friends is punctuated with sporadic outbursts by Job regarding his condition, as he questions God's motives and actions. He was ready to demand of God an explanation: Why this? Why that? Why did You let this happen to me? I demand to speak to You!

In chapter 38, God breaks His silence with words that are as piercing as they are true:

> *Then the* LORD *answered Job out of the whirlwind*

*and said: "Who is this that darkens counsel by words
without knowledge? Dress for action like a man; I will
question you, and you make it known to me.*

*"Where were you when I laid the foundation of
the earth? Tell me, if you have understanding. Who
determined its measurements — surely you know! Or
who stretched the line upon it? On what were its bases
sunk, or who laid its cornerstone, when the morning
stars sang together and all the sons of God shouted for
joy?"* (Job 38:1–7).

You can feel the sting of the rebuke. But even to a man grieving from the loss of all of his children and suffering from
open sores, God softens none of the truth with sympathy
or explanation. As we read chapters 38 through 41, God
continues to grill Job with a series of questions. They are
questions with obvious answers and God uses them to put
Job sternly back into his place in the divine order. Do you
know this, Job? What about this, what about that…? God
uses example after example to finally bring Job to the point
in Job 42 where we read:

*Then Job answered the LORD and said: "I know
that you can do all things, and that no purpose of yours
can be thwarted. 'Who is this that hides counsel without knowledge?' Therefore I have uttered what I did
not understand, things too wonderful for me, which I
did not know. 'Hear, and I will speak; I will question
you, and you make it known to me.' I had heard of
you by the hearing of the ear, but now my eye sees you;*

therefore I despise myself, and repent in dust and ashes"
(Job 42:1–6).

These are the words of a person who finally recognized his
place before his Father, and bowed the knee to His complete
and sovereign authority over all things. God is God; Job is
not. Job acknowledged (as we must) that compared to what
God knows, he knew nothing ... and he repented of his
human arrogance, totally submitting his life to the all-know-
ing, all-powerful God of the universe. Job learned the lesson
the hard way, but he learned it, nonetheless. Finally, he recognized the truth of Isaiah 55:8–9:

> *For my thoughts are not your thoughts, neither are
> your ways my ways, declares the LORD. For as the heav-
> ens are higher than the earth, so are my ways higher
> than your ways and my thoughts than your thoughts.*

What did Job recognize? Job recognized that he was just dust.
Compared to God, he was nothing but a finite and foolish
human being. He recognized that God is God, and that He
knows what He is doing — even when Job was entirely incapable of understanding. And that's really the answer at the
end of the Book of Job. You can cry out to God; you can
plead with Him. But the ultimate answer to it all is to let
God be God. God never did reveal all the details to Job as to
what was behind Job's suffering and loss. As far as we know,
God offered no apology and no explanation. Only when he
stepped into eternity would Job finally learn why God had
ordained such an awful season of suffering and death. But
like Esther, Job's journey is recorded in the Bible to teach all
of us more about ourselves and our God.

Don't argue with God. Let God be God. Bend your knee in submission, obedience, and worship. This is the answer to the issue of death and suffering during the seasons when our faith is stretched to its limit and then pushed beyond.

I praise the Lord for the faith my mother showed during her season of darkness and doubt. She pleaded and pleaded in tears with the Lord to intervene for Rob. I praise the Lord even more that, even though Rob's condition continued to worsen, my mother's faith and trust in God did not wane but grew. In spite of what she could see, in spite of the pain and agony that tore at her heart, she recognized that God was God, and she was not. He was good and was in total control of the situation. And though He chose, according to His eternal purposes, not to intervene and heal, Mum knew that He cared, that He was there, and that He heard the prayers of a grieving mother.

I never once saw my mother get angry at God over what happened. And even though she grieved with a broken heart, her faith in God never wavered. She never waned in being a bold witness for the Lord. And even in her waning years, as she was confined to a bed and wheelchair in a nursing home, she would do all she could to tell both the residents and staff about God's Word and the gospel. In her mid-eighties, Mum had an immune disease that resulted in her losing the use of her leg muscles. She suffered quite a bit with this, really struggled during her last two years. When anyone would ask her about her health she would say, "I had 90 good years." She died just three months before her 92nd birthday. Yes, those last two weren't good. But she never lost her enthusiasm to tell people about the Lord.

She often told me that she was so frustrated she lost her ability to walk, but she praised God that He allowed her to have her mind. And as we sat by her bedside for those few days in November 2019, I saw her frail body, but I could hear her say as she taught us so often as children, "it's only what is done for Jesus that lasts." I've never forgotten that. I could also hear her saying, "Always remember, God first, others second, yourself last." I've never forgotten that either. She was such a bold witness at the nursing home, and a number of residents, as incapacitated as they were, asked to be taken to her memorial service in the church she attended until she had to stay in the nursing home. At the end of the service, so many people came and said something like, "Your mother was such a godly woman. She was so bold with her faith. She impacted so many people. She was inspiring." Others would tell me, "Your mother changed my life. I will never forget her." And now she is with my father and her beloved son, Rob.

In his audio recorded sermon, Rob preached about Job, but he could just as well have been preaching about himself:

> You know that we must realize that Job's suffering was part of God's plan. That's what it was. It must also be true for many people today who suffer so badly, and through it all, you see Job learned the necessity of submitting to the Lord's sovereign purpose, no matter what the cost might be.

Sometimes God has asked people to sacrifice greatly so that His sovereign purposes of redemption and necessary judgment could be carried out. We've already looked at how

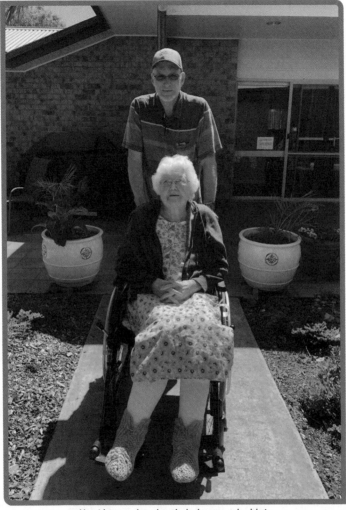

Me with my mother when she had to use a wheelchair.

God orchestrated the death of Esther's parents in order to save the Jewish nation. We saw how the unjust treatment of Joseph was used by God to divert a famine. Ezekiel was told that for God's purposes in dealing with the Jews, his wife — whom he loved so much — was going to be taken away from him:

> *"Son of man, behold, I am about to take the delight of your eyes away from you at a stroke; yet you shall not mourn or weep, nor shall your tears run down"* (Ezekiel 24:16).

During trials like that, the good promised in Romans 8:28 may seem distant and farfetched. In those moments we have two options:

1) either we walk away and deny Him,

2) or we humbly bend the knee, trusting that He will provide the faith we need to make it through. This increased faith brings us into greater intimacy and dependence on God, and this increased level of trust is one of the common purposes in the trials He places in our paths. As Rob said in his sermon, quoting J.I. Packer:

> The ultimate reason from our standpoint why God fills our lives with troubles and perplexities of one sort and another, is to ensure that we shall learn to hold Him fast.

The reason why the Bible spends so much of its time reiterating that God is a strong rock, a firm defense, a sure refuge, and a help for the weak, is because God is bringing home to us that we are weak — mentally, spiritually, and morally. We dare not trust ourselves to find or to follow the right road. God wants us to feel that our way through life is rough and perplexing so that we may learn to lean on Him. Therefore, He takes steps to drive us out of self-confidence, to trust in Himself.

Here, then, we begin to see one of God's great and eternal purposes for our ongoing suffering: pain and death cause us to look to God in dependence — a merciful response to the independence we seek through sin. This is, indeed, a central theme of the Word of God. As Rob taught along these lines, he would often quote passages such as 2 Corinthians 1:3–11:

> *Blessed be the God and Father of our Lord Jesus Christ, the Father of mercies and God of all comfort, who comforts us in all our affliction, so that we may be able to comfort those who are in any affliction, with the comfort with which we ourselves are comforted by God. For as we share abundantly in Christ's sufferings, so through Christ we share abundantly in comfort too. If we are afflicted, it is for your comfort and salvation; and if we are comforted, it is for your comfort, which you experience when you patiently endure the same sufferings that we suffer. Our hope for you is unshaken, for we know that as you share in our sufferings, you will also share in our comfort.*
>
> *For we do not want you to be unaware, brothers, of the affliction we experienced in Asia. For we were so*

> *utterly burdened beyond our strength that we despaired*
> *of life itself. Indeed, we felt that we had received the*
> *sentence of death. But that was to make us rely not on*
> *ourselves but on God who raises the dead. He delivered*
> *us from such a deadly peril, and he will deliver us. On*
> *him we have set our hope that he will deliver us again.*
> *You also must help us by prayer, so that many will give*
> *thanks on our behalf for the blessing granted us through*
> *the prayers of many.*

Rob wanted people to understand that even though we must live with the consequences of sin in this physical universe, God loves us so much that He will provide the comfort necessary for us to cope with the various situations in which we find ourselves.

Hebrews 11:1–2 says, *Now faith is the assurance of things hoped for, the conviction of things not seen. For by it the people of old received their commendation.* So, ultimately, as we read in Hebrews 11:6, *And without faith it is impossible to please him* [God].

There will always be a faith aspect to every area of life. This is true during trials, and it is true as we study origins as well. As I lecture on the topic of creation and evolution, I explain to people that no one can scientifically prove creation or Noah's Flood; nor can anyone prove evolution and millions of years, for that matter, as none of us were there to witness these events. Both worldviews require faith. However, the Bible's account of origins in Genesis builds a worldview that does make sense of the evidence in the world around us, and observational science confirms the biblical record.

For example, Genesis tells us that God created distinct kinds of animals and plants according to their kinds with the inference that they reproduce within those kinds. The science of genetics confirms that no new genetic information is produced from matter, and animals and plants reproduce their own kind, even though there can be great variation (even speciation) within a kind because of the variety in the genes.

This is the point: only the God of the Bible is omniscient, omnipotent, and omnipresent, and the bottom line is that we are not. We are not going to have all the answers to everything all the time. Although we have answers to many questions concerning the origins issue, there are those we just can't answer as we don't know everything. This side of the grave, we may never know why things like Rob's sickness have happened. Only God knows. We are nothing but fallen mortal human beings who, like Job, need to recognize that we know nothing compared to what God knows. When we can't see the good, we walk on in faith through the revealed truth of God's Word.

Submission to God is never easy, and it always goes against the nature of our sinful flesh. The challenge to repent and submit as Job did is more difficult when we feel like a victim. During difficult times, we are also likely to feel used or abandoned. In these moments of deep trial, we feel we need the comfort of God the most, yet these may be the days when we sense it the least … and must choose by an act of our wills to obey and submit to God's purposes.

Philip Yancey comments on this type of faith:

> I hesitate to say this, because it is a hard truth and one I do not want to acknowledge, but Job stands as merely the most extreme example of what appears to be a universal law of faith. The kind of faith God values seems to develop best when everything fuzzes over, when God stays silent, when the fog rolls in.[1]

When "the fog" becomes so thick that we can't see any of the good God promises, we have no choice but to return to His written and living Word to give us the full, big picture of what is going on around us. God's Word tells us clearly where death and sickness originated. We understand we live in a fallen world. Each of us needs to recognize that we are sinful creatures living under a curse because of sin, and that death for every human being is both inevitable and imminent. Through Christ and the Cross, every person can be spiritually healed, but total healing won't come until we leave this sin-cursed universe. Yet here and now, God has a sovereign plan far greater than we could imagine, but we may not be able to see it or understand it at all. We don't know everything — in fact, we know nothing compared to God. We need to learn the lesson Job learned.

The question, then, becomes this: Do we put our faith in the Word of an all-powerful God, who knows everything and has always been there? Or do we place our faith in the words of fallible humans who don't know everything, who

---

1. Philip Yancey, *Disappointment with God* (Grand Rapids, MI: Zondervan, 1988), p. 204.

haven't always been there, and whose values and subjective thinking lead only to fatalism? The answer to that question is repentance and submission to God and His perfect will. As Eli said to Samuel, *"It is the LORD. Let him do what seems good to him"* (1 Samuel 3:18).

I believe that if Rob could speak to us right now, he would remind us of those great people of faith remembered in the Book of Hebrews who *suffered mocking and flogging, and even chains and imprisonment. They were stoned, they were sawn in two, they were killed with the sword. They went about in skins of sheep and goats, destitute, afflicted, mistreated* (Hebrews 11:36–37).

These people now look down on us *as a great cloud of witnesses* to see how we will run this race of life (Hebrews 12:1). By faith, they all took their place in God's plan. Rob, in the normal course of events in this fallen world, was allowed to suffer a terrible disease … and has now joined their ranks. Will we choose to do the same?

21

Now, But Not Yet

I had been listening to Rob's sermon tape for about 40 minutes ... and he was still on a roll. The fervency and the certainty with which he spoke painted an audible image of the brother I once had. It was very surreal. He sounded like the Rob that I knew; he sounded real, but I had to remind myself that the disease had by now taken almost everything that he had been when the sermon was recorded.

Rob had covered a lot of material in this one tape, and the message was saturated with vibrant passion, solid content, and practical application. He had covered the issues of sin, answering with solid biblical support the question that asked, "Why does suffering and death exist in a world with a good and loving God?" He had investigated the issues of physical healing and the "normal" course of human life in a fallen world ... a course that included the inevitability of sickness, suffering, and death. He had expounded on the implications of Christ and the Cross, illuminating how that perfect sacrifice of God had paid the price for sin.

What a big difference when you can stand back and give people a big picture of history, I thought. When we understand the beauty and perfection of Eden, and how sin changed everything, we are forced to be consistent when we talk about good and bad, and right and wrong. Biblical history clearly brings each individual to a point where he or she must accept or reject the gospel. Each must either receive Christ's sacrifice and forgiveness or turn away from Him for eternity. Wow. What a difference a truthful perspective makes. Rather than leading to fatalism and despair, believing in the history of Genesis gives us the foundation on which to build answers to these most probing of human issues.

This is why at the Creation Museum (and Ark Encounter) I told our script writers for all the teaching signs for the various exhibits that we needed to give the big picture of history from Genesis to Revelation. Most people don't really have that big picture so they can then build the right way of thinking (put on the correct glasses) to then have the ability to understand the world correctly.

I have seen many Christian leaders on television who have no solid answers to the questions surrounding death and suffering. They say things like, "You just have to trust," or "You just have to have faith. We don't know why these things occurred." But you know why I believe that they can't

Creation Museum

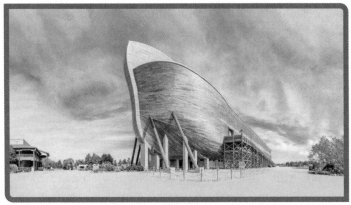

The Ark Encounter

give answers? It's because they don't believe the Book of Genesis (or aren't sure what to believe about it) as Rob did and we do at Answers in Genesis. They don't believe God's Word as they should. They have been influenced by the world so they don't have this history that they can use to explain sin, death, and disease to the world. And so they can't give answers. It is only those who believe the history God has given to us (beginning in Genesis 1:1) who can consistently explain how there can be a loving God and death, suffering, and disease at the same time. As finite beings, we can't give ultimate and absolute answers in regard to everything, but we can give answers that are consistent, logical, rational, and defensible as we search the Scriptures for solutions.

As Rob tried to conclude his sermon on the tape, I smiled as he kept apologizing to the congregation because his message was going overtime. Yes, he was sorry — but not so sorry that he was willing to stop! He still had many things to say and was unable to restrain the words that were on his heart. They were words from the Word of God that could bring hope and eternal perspective to his church … and to us now years away from where he was. His passion for the Bible again overflowed as he turned his focus to the future. He began expounding on two things: first, the things that are reality in our lives now (now that we are in Christ); and second, the things that are not yet (the realities that await us on the other side of the grave when all things are made new again).

With his customary flair for words, he described the awkward balance in which we find ourselves as we navigate through life somewhere between "the Fall" and the coming "consummation" of history when Christ will return and all things will be restored. He had covered past history, explaining how we got to where we are in the present. Now he was explaining coming history, instructing how we are to move ahead, living out our place in the biblical "big picture" as it spans toward the future.

I firmly believe that if Rob could talk to us today, he would tell us that he is restored and healed from the worst disease: sin. When Christ was on earth, He carried out great miracles, including wonderful physical healings of sick people. As significant as those healings were, Rob preached that "the Great Physician" had a broader focus of restoration in mind. Rob said:

> When the Lord Jesus came, His whole purpose and reason was to pay the penalty for our sin, to appease the wrath of God, and to rise again from the dead. His whole purpose was to make us what He intends us to be. What does He intend us to be? Well, you see, He is speaking there about freedom for the prisoners, sight for the blind, release of the oppressed. It means this: He paid for our sins; He bought us forgiveness. That's what it's all about, real and genuine forgiveness so that He could bring us into a right relationship with God, with the Lord Jesus Christ.

Rob explained this further by expounding the passage in Isaiah 53:5 which states, *But he was pierced for our transgressions; he was crushed for our iniquities; upon him was the chastisement that brought us peace, and with his wounds we are healed.*

Moving on to 1 Peter 2:22–24, he showed how this passage gives us the correct understanding of the Isaiah passage:

> *He committed no sin, neither was deceit found in his mouth. When he was reviled, he did not revile in return; when he suffered, he did not threaten, but*

continued entrusting himself to him who judges justly.
He himself bore our sins in his body on the tree, that
we might die to sin and live to righteousness. By his
wounds you have been healed.

As Rob preached on this particular passage, both the content
of the passage and the importance of interpreting it properly
became evident as he said:

> What's the context here? That's what we have to
> examine. Let's put the Bible back in context, because
> a lot of people take verses out of context and they
> will just apply them to whatever they want. But the
> context here is this — that Peter is talking about the
> death of the Lord Jesus Christ for our sins. That's the
> whole emphasis and that's what he gets out of Isaiah
> 53. In fact, when it says "and by his wounds you have
> been healed," the Greek makes it clear that "you have
> been healed" is in the passive tense. It means you
> have already been healed. Friends, you are all healed.
> The Bible tells us that if you are in the Lord Jesus
> Christ, Christ died to shed His blood so that you can
> be washed clean from your sin. That's the whole per-
> spective of it. That's what it means. That's the context
> of it all. You already have been healed. You already
> have been washed clean from your sin. You have
> been restored to Christ, and it's now and not yet.
> Now we have the cleansing and forgiveness. Yet to
> come is a new heaven and new earth in which there
> will be no sicknesses and no death. But the primary
> emphasis is definitely not on physical healing now.

Our primary focus here is on the Lord Jesus Christ
and His death and Resurrection for us. That's what
that verse means. In fact, we know that the Lord
Jesus went out and healed people; He went out cast-
ing out evil spirits; He went out raising people from
the dead. He did that. He stopped the storm, didn't
He? Remember that? In all of this, the Lord Jesus
is showing us that our restoration is to be spiritual.
That's what He is talking about, that's what He is
showing us. That our restoration is spiritual now.
Right now. Right now, you and I, through the Lord
Jesus Christ, are spiritually restored to God. Right
now, through the Lord Jesus, through His death and
His Resurrection. But you see, it is now and not yet.
It is yet to come.... We are living in a world where
we are living now and not yet. Now we are spiritually
restored to God, spiritually restored through the
Lord Jesus Christ, yes, but it is yet to come. What
is yet to come? What is yet to come is a new heaven
and a new earth. That is what we are looking forward
to. And in fact, that is where our focus needs to be,
friends, because in the new heaven and the new earth
the Lord Jesus, who is righteousness, will dwell there,
and we shall dwell with Him. Isn't that fantastic? We
don't want to focus on this world; it's a world ruined
by sin. We don't want to focus on ourselves; we are
people who have been ruined by sin. We want to
focus on the new heaven and the new earth that is
yet to come. In that new heaven and new earth, there
will be no sickness; there will be no disease; there will

be no demons; there will be no death; there will be no chaos. Everything is going to be peaceful and perfect. Wonderful, isn't it? You see, now and not yet. Restored to Christ today, yes — and yet to come is all that we are looking forward to in the new heaven and the new earth.

In fact, you see the New Testament emphasis is not primarily on physical healing, but it is on the power of the Holy Spirit who brings us into a right relationship with the Lord Jesus Christ. That is the primary aspect of the New Testament. Right now, this spiritual healing from sin is about relationship, a trusting relationship that is more valuable than anything else on earth. Paul put this into words in Philippians 3:8–11:

> *Indeed, I count everything as loss because of the surpassing worth of knowing Christ Jesus my Lord. For his sake I have suffered the loss of all things and count them as rubbish, in order that I may gain Christ and be found in him, not having a righteousness of my own that comes from the law, but that which comes through faith in Christ, the righteousness from God that depends on faith — that I may know him and the power of his resurrection, and may share his sufferings, becoming like him in his death, that by any means possible I may attain the resurrection from the dead.*

That relationship starts at the moment Christ comes into our spirits and is cultivated until death. As Rob said, it is now, but not yet. Yet to come is the final consummation of all things, a complete and total healing for the soul and the body and the world that ushers in a new and never-ending era of unhindered intimacy with the Creator. We read in 1 Corinthians 13:12: *For now we see in a mirror dimly, but then face to face. Now I know in part; then I shall know fully, even as I have been fully known.*

The Bible tells us that sometime in the future we will see a restoring of the harmony that existed in Eden once again. Acts 3:18–21 speaks of this restoration and where it fits in the big picture:

> *But what God foretold by the mouth of all the prophets, that his Christ would suffer, he thus fulfilled. Repent therefore, and turn back, that your sins may be blotted out, that times of refreshing may come from the presence of the Lord, and that he may send the Christ appointed for you, Jesus, whom heaven must receive until the time for restoring all the things about which God spoke by the mouth of his holy prophets long ago.*

Note that God is going to restore, and He is going to make all things new again. The standard to which we will return is the one that existed so long ago in Eden. Everything will be in balance once again — the groaning of creation will cease and the righteousness that is equated with peace and harmony with the animals and man will be the norm again, just as it was before sin.

Might I ask, however, where we would be without this foundation of hope? From Genesis we are able to see the picture of how things were, telling us also something of how they will be. Only from the perfection of the past can we tangibly hope in the promise of this glorious future. Those who reject a literal Genesis have little to go on and will probably never understand the believer's hope — the hope that life will again be as perfect as it once was, but no longer is. How can there be a restoration to such a perfect state when there never was one to start with? That's why believing in millions of years of death and suffering before man sinned doesn't make sense and doesn't fit with God's Word. Without this understanding of original perfection (before sin), there is no longing for heaven, just a grim outlook on life, lack of true joy, and the beginning of a steady slide into spiritual bankruptcy and lukewarmness.

The existence of Eden, as long ago as it was (approximately 6,000 years ago), gives hope for the future. Between now and then, in a world where death and sin are "normal," this hope gives us faith to face another day. I believe we are incapable of imagining what heaven will be like, just as we are unable to truly imagine what life was like in Eden before the Fall. We do know that there will be no curse (Revelation 22:3). In this present sin-cursed world, we live in sin-ravaged bodies that cause us to groan. But what an encouragement to know that Christ will one day restore our bodies, and the whole creation, to perfection!

We see a glimpse of the complete healing of all creation that will take place through the ministry of Christ and the Apostles. Of course, we wish this would happen now — and at times, for His purposes, God does ordain specific miraculous events to overcome the consequences of the Curse. But at the right time, God will bring this present era to a close, this great season of suffering and death will end — and then, for all those who do trust in Him, we will have that final healing. Yes, we have a fraction of it now, but the completeness of it is not yet.

But that leads to a reminder of what I mentioned earlier in the book. Sadly, many Christians and Christian leaders have accepted the belief in millions of years for the universe, earth, and fossil record. They have accepted the secular worldview (based on naturalism) that the fossil record was supposedly laid down millions of years before man.

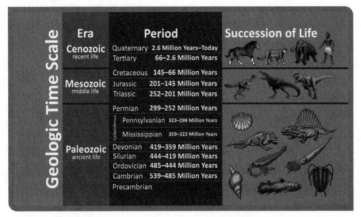

In the fossil record we see death of animals, diseases (like cancer, arthritis, abscesses, etc.) in bones and evidence animals were eating each other. After God created man, He said everything He created was *very good* (Genesis 1:31). This means if one believes in millions of years, then one is stating that God said diseases like cancer are "very good." It also means God — not our sin — is responsible for death and disease. Therefore, what did the Fall do? And if death, disease, and suffering has always existed, what would the restoration be? Is the restoration going to be full of death, suffering, and disease? But God's Word says in the new heavens and new earth, *He will wipe away every tear from their eyes, and death shall be no more, neither shall there be mourning, nor crying, nor pain anymore, for the former things have passed away* (Revelation 21:4).

And if death existed millions of years before man sinned, then what has the death and Resurrection of Jesus Christ got to do with sin? Really, believing in millions of years is an attack on God's character and undermines the gospel.

Between Now and Then

Look carefully then how you walk, not as unwise but as wise, making the best use of the time, because the days are evil (Ephesians 5:15–16).

Living as we are now (between "the Fall" and "the consummation"), how then should we live? In the above verse, Paul challenges us to live lives of wisdom and careful progression. These would be lives that are lived in truth, trust, and with a vision for eternity.

John 8:32 says, *you will know the truth, and the truth will set you free*. This certainly is the case when dealing with origins and the big picture of biblical history (including a proper understanding of Eden, the fall, Christ, and the Cross, and the restoration that will consummate all things). The truth about the inevitability of death sets us free as well. Because of what we know through the revealed Word of God, we no longer need to be bound by the fear of death. Having received the gospel, we can even be expectant and looking forward to what lies beyond the grave. Where do we find such truth? Jesus Himself is truth (John 14:6), and the Bible, we must always remember, is truth as well (Psalm 119:160). Devotion to its study and upholding its authority is central to living a life of wisdom. And God's Word stands forever.

> *The grass withers, the flower fades when the breath*
> *of the LORD blows on it; surely the people are grass. The*
> *grass withers, the flower fades, but the word of our God*
> *will stand forever* (Isaiah 40:7–8).

A life of wisdom is also built on trust. We are to trust in God as the Creator and sustainer of all existence, trust in His immediate presence in our lives, and trust in His continued provision as we seek to live lives of faith in the midst of suffering and death.

> *But he said to me, "My grace is sufficient for you,*
> *for my power is made perfect in weakness." Therefore I*
> *will boast all the more gladly of my weaknesses, so that*
> *the power of Christ may rest upon me. For the sake*
> *of Christ, then, I am content with weaknesses, insults,*
> *hardships, persecutions, and calamities. For when I am*
> *weak, then I am strong"* (2 Corinthians 12:9–10).

Wisdom dictates that you not only trust in Him, but that you also trust in who the Scriptures say you now are in Christ. Between now and death, it will always be a challenge to remember that the very presence of God is not just with you but is within you (John 14:17). Continually, you will need to renew your minds according to the biblical fact that you have been crucified with Him and it is no longer you who live, but Christ who lives in you (Galatians 2:20). When it is time to submit and obey, you must be wise to recognize that God's Spirit Himself gives you the power and the desire to do what is right (John 15:5; Philippians 4:13).

Again, in those times when wisdom fails and circumstances tear at your heart … when the tears will not cease, and the grief will not lift … in those times there will always be the need to bow the knee before God as your only sovereign King and trust Him in spite of all that you see and all that you feel. Then you can make wise and godly decisions in this fallen world. We read in Deuteronomy 30:19–20 how the Israelites were offered a choice by God; it's the same choice that you have day by day:

> *"I call heaven and earth to witness against you today, that I have set before you life and death, blessing and curse. Therefore choose life, that you and your offspring may live, loving the Lord your God, obeying his voice and holding fast to him…."*

Finally, wisdom requires a vision for eternity. We simply must accept the reality of our mortality and live lives for the things that will never end. The Bible tells us something that science knows very well: *The years of our life are seventy, or even by reason of strength eighty; yet their span is but toil and trouble; they are soon gone, and we fly away* (Psalm 90:10).

We consider someone who lives to 80 years old to have had a long life. However, contemplate this: how long is 80 compared to eternity? Job 8:9 says, *For we are but of yesterday and know nothing, for our days on earth are a shadow.*

Even though we live in time (and to us the sufferings of a loved one like Rob seem so prolonged), compared to eternity it's not even a fleeting moment. That does not in any way negate the trauma of it all in this life, but we do need to put it all in perspective and try to see more of the "big picture" as God has revealed it in the Bible.

Suffering and death from sin is the universal norm, and that should be a warning to us — a reminder that our days are numbered. If we are wise, we will invest the best of all our resources for things with eternal significance.

> *Do not lay up for yourselves treasures on earth, where moth and rust destroy and where thieves break in and steal, but lay up for yourselves treasures in heaven, where neither moth nor rust destroys and where thieves do not break in and steal. For where your treasure is, there your heart will be also* (Matthew 6:19–21).

> *Lift up your eyes to the heavens, and look at the earth beneath; for the heavens vanish like smoke, the earth will wear out like a garment, and they who dwell in it will die in like manner; but my salvation will be forever, and my righteousness will never be dismayed* (Isaiah 51:6).

How important it is to put our trust in the living and inerrant Word of God and live for worthy purposes. Think about this! Eventually, you will die for what you are living for, since eventually, you will die. It's not a matter of *if* you will die (we know that is a certainty). It's a matter of living for a cause that is worth dying for.

> *For truly, I say to you, until heaven and earth pass away, not an iota, not a dot, will pass from the Law until all is accomplished* (Matthew 5:18).

> *But I do not account my life of any value nor as precious to myself, if only I may finish my course and the ministry that I received from the Lord Jesus, to testify to the gospel of the grace of God* (Acts 20:24).

From Genesis to Revelation

In the beginning, we know that God created the heavens and the earth, and then man and woman. When He was done, He said it was all exceptionally good. Sin has polluted it all, but still a remnant remains … a shattered reflection of the pure good that once was. That's why we see a world of beauty and ugliness, a world of life and death, a world of joy and sorrow. All seems so contradictory but can be understood in terms of a perfect world now marred by sin. We are living in a once beautiful perfect world now groaning because of the effects of our sin.

Between the once perfect world and the new heaven and the new earth, we will live for an unknown duration of time. In the Book of Revelation, chapters 21 and 22, God gives the Apostle John a vision for what will emerge from the disease, destruction, and death of the present days. The descriptions paint a picture of the future that awaits us. Both the parallels and the contrast between what once was and what will be are important:

> And I heard a loud voice from the throne saying, "Behold, the dwelling place of God is with man. He will dwell with them, and they will be his people, and God himself will be with them as their God. He will wipe away every tear from their eyes, and death shall be no more, neither shall there be mourning, nor crying,

nor pain anymore, for the former things have passed away" (Revelation 21:3–4).

Then the angel showed me the river of the water of life, bright as crystal, flowing from the throne of God and of the Lamb through the middle of the street of the city; also, on either side of the river, the tree of life with its twelve kinds of fruit, yielding its fruit each month. The leaves of the tree were for the healing of the nations (Revelation 22:1–2).

The new heaven and the new earth: This is the great hope for all who suffer in this fallen world. This is the hope God leaves us in the closing chapters of the Bible … and this is the hope that Rob left his congregation at the end of his sermon. As I turned off the recording, I realized that he had recorded this sermon only a few months before "frontal lobe dementia" began to make him an extreme illustration to his own message.

Jesus Wept

Jesus wept (John 11:35) is the shortest verse in many translations of the Bible. This verse is part of the account of the death, burial, and resurrection of Lazarus. I've often thought about why Jesus wept when He stood before the tomb of Lazarus.

Perhaps He wept at death itself. As we know, the Scriptures call death an *enemy*. One day death itself will be thrown into the lake of fire. Death is a judgment because of sin, and it causes such grief. Jesus knew what a horrible thing death is but also knew how bad sin is and it had to be dealt with.

Maybe He wept knowing He would have to die an agonizing death soon because of our sin but to provide a way of salvation for us. He knew how horrible His death would be

Jesus raises Lazarus

and what it would entail paying the penalty for sin. In fact, after the last supper, we read that Jesus went to the Garden of Gethsemane on the Mount of Olives where He agonized over the coming crucifixion:

> *And he came out and went, as was his custom, to the Mount of Olives, and the disciples followed him. And when he came to the place, he said to them, "Pray that you may not enter into temptation." And he withdrew from them about a stone's throw, and knelt down and prayed, saying, "Father, if you are willing, remove this cup from me. Nevertheless, not my will, but yours, be done." And there appeared to him an angel from heaven, strengthening him. And being in agony he prayed more earnestly; and his sweat became like great drops of blood falling down to the ground* (Luke 22:39–44).

It's also possible He wept because He knew so many of the Jewish religious leaders were so rebellious, rejecting Jesus as

First-century Jerusalem

the Messiah, that even when Lazarus was raised from the dead, they would try to kill Lazarus to get rid of the evidence of this resurrection:

So the chief priests made plans to put Lazarus to death as well (John 12:10).

Maybe Jesus wept as He knew the Jewish leaders would call for His crucifixion and the people would cry out, *His blood be on us and on our children!* (Matthew 27:25). And on top of this knowing the awful, gruesome destruction coming upon Jerusalem as it did in A.D. 70 because of their rebellion. And Jesus also knew those who reject Him will be separated from Him for eternity in a place of judgment. He surely wept over this.

Jesus had also previously wept over Jerusalem:

And when he drew near and saw the city, he wept over it saying, "Would that you, even you, had known on this day the things that make for peace! But now they are hidden from your eyes. For the days will come

upon you, when your enemies will set up a barricade
around you and surround you and hem you in on every
side and tear you down to the ground, you and your
children within you. And they will not leave one stone
upon another in you, because you did not know the
time of your visitation" (Luke 19:41–44).

No wonder He would weep knowing all this, having previously said, *"O Jerusalem, Jerusalem, the city that kills the*
prophets and stones those who are sent to it! How often would I
have gathered your children together as a hen gathers her brood
under her wings, and you were not willing!" (Matthew 23:37).

Perhaps He wept because as the Godman, he was 100%
God, but 100% human as well, so He showed compassion
to Mary and Martha and the others, grieving with them.

Maybe He wept because He understood the horrible
separation resulting from death. We grieve over that horrible separation from a loved one, even though we know for
Christians we will be united in heaven one day.

He may have wept knowing He would raise Lazarus
from the dead, but Lazarus would have to go through the
valley of the shadow of death again in the future.

And perhaps He wept knowing the separation our sin
caused from us and our Creator and the resulting judgment
of death.

Jesus wept at death and we weep at death.

> *Wretched man that I am! Who will deliver me*
> *from this body of death?* (Romans 7:24).

25

Life or Death

When God created a garden for Adam and Eve, the first two people, to live in, He placed two special trees in this garden — the Tree of Life and the Tree of the Knowledge of Good and Evil. I call the Tree of the Knowledge of Good and Evil a "Tree of Death." God warned Adam that if he ate of this tree, he would *surely die*.

Adam chose the Tree of Death. When Adam rebelled, sin entered the world, and as a result of sin, God judged with death. Really, the Tree of Death and the Tree of Life represent the battle that has been raging for six thousand years. It's a battle between:

- Those who don't obey God's Word and those who do
- Man's word and God's Word

199

- Darkness and light
- Evil and good
- Those who scatter and those who gather
- Those who are against Christ and those who are for Him
- The ones who build their lives on the sand and those who build their lives on the rock
- Those who don't receive the free gift of salvation and those who do
- The devil and Christ

This war has been raging ever since Adam disobeyed God.

Now God's Son has already won this war when He died on the Cross, but was raised from the dead thus conquering death. I call the Cross a "Tree of Life." The first Adam through his life brought death into the world. Jesus, who is called the *last Adam,* through His death, brings life to those who will receive the free gift of salvation He offers.

That is what is before us today. Put your faith and trust

GOD'S WAY BACK TO THE TREE OF LIFE

in what Christ did on the Tree of Life, or put your faith and trust in man's word that rejects God, which really is a "Tree of Death." In our modern world, man's supposed justification for rejecting God and the Tree of Life, is Darwin's evolutionary tree. This tree is a Tree of Death, as he proposed that time and death brought man into existence, and death will be the end.

This reminds me of what God put before the people in Jeremiah's day:

> *And to this people you shall say: "Thus says the LORD: Behold, I set before you the way of life and the way of death. He who stays in this city shall die by the sword, by famine, and by pestilence, but he who goes out and surrenders to the Chaldeans who are besieging you shall live and shall have his life as a prize of war"* (Jeremiah 21:8–9).

He was telling the people, if you stay in the city, that seems

a safe place to stay, you will die. But if you surrender, which seems like certain death, you will live. In other words, if you want life, you need to obey God and do what He says, no matter what your human reasoning is telling you.

And that's what is before us today. Trust God's Word for salvation and receive the free gift He offers. Yes, it's hard to understand that while you live in this world you may undergo all sorts of suffering. But you will surely die and then will live in heaven with God forever. If you reject God and trust man's word, you may or may not have all sorts of treasures on this earth, but you will surely die and spend eternity separated from God in what the Bible calls a *second death*.

It's life or death.

> *For the wages of sin is death, but the free gift of God is eternal life in Christ Jesus our Lord* (Romans 6:23).

> *But as for the cowardly, the faithless, the detestable, as for murderers, the sexually immoral, sorcerers, idolaters, and all liars, their portion will be in the lake that burns with fire and sulfur, which is the second death* (Revelation 21:8).

26

The Last "Goodbye"

The last time I saw my brother alive, I sat beside his bed watching my mother lovingly caress his head. "I wish he could just say 'Mum' one more time," she said. Instead, there were times when her son (obviously not knowing what he was doing) would push her away — seemingly to reject the loving hand that gently stroked his cheek.

Robert, not long before the disease ravaged his body.

Unmoved, our mother continued to patiently feed him his favorite drinks, instinctively hoping to satisfy his hunger, perhaps giving him some joy and comfort — if he could even experience such feelings in his embattled state. I looked on with mixed emotion. On the one hand, I wanted to cry. On the other hand, I rejoiced that Rob already had the most important healing of all. His spiritual healing from sin meant when he passed away from this earth, he would be totally healed in eternity. Many memories and many Bible verses passed through my mind in those final minutes with him:

> *For I consider that the sufferings of this present time are not worth comparing with the glory that is to be revealed to us* (Romans 8:18).

> *For this light momentary affliction is preparing for us an eternal weight of glory beyond all comparison* (2 Corinthians 4:17).

Knowing that this would probably be my final goodbye to Robert, I bent over and kissed him on his forehead. "Goodbye, Robert. I love you, brother," I said. I left the room holding back tears, but also departed with a real peace — the kind of peace *which surpasses all understanding* (Philippians 4:7). The tears would come, and then come again and again. Even today, I can't think about him for very long without feeling the loss and reliving portions of the pain. But those emotions I know will one day cease as well, as every tear is wiped away by Jesus … this I know, for the Bible says it is so.

The question has been answered through the big picture of God's holy Word. Why is there suffering and death? Eden was lost to sin. I now live in a fallen world. And we need to let God be God.

One of my favorite preachers of all time, Martyn Lloyd Jones,[1] stated:

> That is Christian teaching. It starts with God. It does not start with modern man or with the latest knowledge. It does not start with biology or geology. It starts by saying, "In the beginning God" — the Creator of the whole universe and the sustainer of the cosmos, God in His holy being, God in His righteousness, His glory, His everlasting light. God! And the world that He made and the men and women that He made. People made in the image of God! Not sniveling creatures going through life just eating and drinking and indulging in sex as if they were animals in the farmyard. No, no; man made upright and righteous, a reflection of something of the divine glory itself. God! Man! The universe! And then the Fall. Adam and Eve's rebellion against God, and consequently sin and shame and havoc and misery and unhappiness, and men and women in need of salvation, and the judgment of God upon it all. This is apostolic teaching.[2]

Now in the future there will be a restoration and a healing that is beyond the imagination. In the meantime, I know that my brother is in the hands of His Creator, as I am … now, but not yet.

---

1. Martyn Lloyd-Jones was a gifted expositional preacher in England in the 20th century who preached in Westminster Chapel in London for 30 years.
2. Martyn Lloyd-Jones, *Acts, 6 volumes in 3* (Wheaton, IL: Crossway Publishing Co., 2015) Chapters 1–8.

For I consider that the sufferings of this present time are not worth comparing with the glory that is to be revealed to us (Romans 8:18).

I held my mother closely as we walked down the hallway, out the door of the nursing home, and toward the car. Around us, people continued about their daily business, boarding buses, coming out of stores with armloads of goods, children laughing on their way home from school … it all looked so normal in the bright sunlight. People were going to and fro, indifferent and unaware of what was happening to my brother Robert. But why should they? They didn't know him or know what was happening to him. Why should they care?

But as I looked at them, I thought of the fact that each one of them is, like Rob, going to face death one day. Many of them may end up in nursing homes, aimlessly staring at the wall, their minds tragically deteriorated from the effects of disease. What is the purpose of all that they are doing now if death is just the end of it all? Is it all, in the end, futility? No, no, it's not.

In fact, it is all full of meaning, guided by the hand of the God who not only created it all, but also causes it all to work together for good — and soon enough He will restore it all once again. We all will die, yes, but we all will live for eternity either in heaven (the renewed creation) with our Creator, or in hell, separated from Him for eternity.

As I thought about this, I felt anew Robert's passion and the burden he felt to warn the world about the true meaning of life and tell them the wonderful saving message of the gospel. That's what Rob would want me to feel, I thought. They need to care — they need to face the reality of death. At the car with my mother, I thought about the fact that one day I'll have to say goodbye to her also … and the fact that I too will someday finish my days on this earth. Until then, suffering and death will be the norm. But after that…

> *There will no longer be any curse; and the throne of God and of the Lamb shall be in it, and His bond-servants shall serve Him; they will see His face, and His name will be on their foreheads. And there will no longer be any night; and they shall not have need of the light of a lamp nor the light of the sun, because the Lord God will illuminate them; and they will reign forever and ever* (Revelation 22:3–5; NASB).

> *He who testifies to these things says, "Surely I am coming soon." Amen. Come, Lord Jesus! The grace of the Lord Jesus be with all. Amen* (Revelation 22:20–21).

Rob passed away on the 9th of June 2002, seven years to the day from when our father passed away on June 9, 1995.

Death a Shadow

On November 15th, 2019, three months before her 92nd birthday, we said goodbye to my mother as she left this earthly life for her heavenly home.

She lived as a widow for over 24 years. She missed my Dad every day of her life during that time. Why did God allow her to suffer this grief? But then, that question can be asked a million times or more of others. She was such a witness to people in her church and in that nursing home. Perhaps she wouldn't have been such a strong witness if she didn't go through this situation. But then again, she was always bold about her faith. Maybe that boldness has been a

My siblings and I saying goodbye to Mum at the nursing home.

Mum's memorial service.

witness to others, and it certainly was to me. And you know what I realized? There's an infinite number of things I don't know about, so just because some things don't make sense to

Saying goodbye to Mum at the graveside.

my finite fallible mind, that doesn't mean there's not a grand plan beyond what I could ever humanly comprehend. Yes, I need to let God be God, even though I miss my parents and my brother so.

But their impact lives on. My brother's impact certainly lives on in this book and in many other ways. My parents' impact lives on in their children's lives, in our own children and their children's lives. And my parents' impact lives on through the ministry of Answers in Genesis, the Ark Encounter, the Creation Museum, and Answers Academy, the Christian school founded by our eldest daughter Renee. And what a legacy to see our children and grandchildren involved in this ministry that is impacting many tens of millions of people each year around the world.

Every time I look at a photo of my mother, I hear her saying as I stated earlier:

It's only what is done for Jesus that lasts.

She drummed that into us as children. I also hear her saying:

God first, others second, yourselves last.

You can tell she greatly impacted me.

Mum and Dad would often take us to North Queensland during school holidays so we could visit Mum's parents who had a sugar cane farm at the foot of Mt. Bartle Frere, the highest mountain in the state of Queensland. We would stay in a tent or caravan (RV) at their old farmhouse. As a young boy I'll never forget my mother telling me about how as a teenager she started a Sunday School and used her bicycle as a "taxi" of sorts to ensure two young girls in the area could attend. This had a great impact on me. I would think, "If my mother did that to make sure these girls were taught God's Word and the gospel, what can I do to reach people with the gospel message?"

Farmhouse (far left) and sugar cane farm at the foot of Mt. Bartle Frere, Nth Qld.

Mum with her mother in the early 60s at Mt. Bartle Frere.

A few years before she passed away, I had the opportunity to interview my mother for a few hours and record this on video. I thought this would be great for our kids and grandkids and generations to come to learn more about the spiritual legacy passed on by my parents. I never thought of doing this with my father, sadly. I made a shortened version of the interview to share with many of our supporters. At one stage she told me the account of taking these girls to her Sunday School. Here is a transcript from the video.

Bicycle Story Part 1:
[Ken] So you got involved in Sunday school in your area, in Bartle Frere.
[Mum] … so there was nothing for the children. First

of all, I went to my mother, and I said I'd like to be a
missionary, you know, and she said she couldn't part with
me. She said, "Why don't you be a missionary in your
own district?"

[Ken] How old were you then?

[Mum] I can't remember, a teenager. So anyway, I went
around all the houses and said I was gonna start a Sunday
school on Sunday. So, there was 30 kids turned up on
that Sunday.

[Ken] Where'd you hold it?

[Mum] Bartle Frere Hall.

[Ken] How far away was that from where you lived?

[Mum] About a mile. But then the other thing was, there
were two little girls at Pawngilly, about a mile the other
direction. And they were upset because they couldn't
come. They were only little. So, I thought, okay. So, I got
my father's bike, tied a cushion on the handlebars. And
so, I'd ride up to Pawngilly on my bike, and I put one on
the bar and one on the handlebar, and I'd ride right back
down to the Bartle Frere Hall.

[Ken] So you'd ride a mile up to their house, collect them
—

[Mum] My house, and then back to the Bartle Frere, and
then two miles back to the hall. Then back home.

[Ken] And then two miles to take them back home, and
then a mile to go back home yourself?

[Mum] Well, I did that for … I can't remember how long
I did it for, until one day their father says, "I better do

something about this." So, he started running them to Sunday school. I know I did it for a long time.

[Ken] Like months or a year, or?

[Mum] Oh … months. I can't remember, Kenny.

[Ken] So you had 30 people turn up. I didn't know that you started a Sunday school back then.

[Mum] I had 30 kids turned up. But the funny part about it, they were from this high to teenagers. I thought, "Wow, what do I do with these?"

[Ken] So what did you do?

[Mum] I got a couple of parents to come and help me, and they were very good. So, I took all the little ones and they took the bigger ones.

[Ken] So you were really missionary-minded right from a young child.

[Mum] Very much so. When I was only little, I just used to sit on the floor and try to make up sermons….

[Ken] And that's because of the training of your parents?

[Mum] Oh, yes.

Bicycle Story Part 2 about those same two girls:

[Mum] A few years ago, they had a reunion at Bartle Frere School, quite a few years ago, and I went to it. And Beth ran up to me, I didn't know her, and she asked me if I knew her. And she's talking, "Do you know me?" "Oh, no." And she said, "I'm Beth Persky, remember me? I'm a Christian and I still love the Lord." I said, "Oh, that's lovely." And her little sister came up and said, "Oh, I've gone away from the Lord, but I promise I'll come back."

[Ken] And was it that Sunday school that really helped with that, do you think?

[Mum] Yeah, yeah.

[Ken] Because you put them on the bicycle handle and took them to Sunday school.

[Mum] … so I met them that few years back and that's what happened. It's interesting, isn't it?

[Ken] Yeah, it is interesting.

[Mum] But see there, if you plant the seed, that's what happens.

We have several funny stories about Mum in her old age, but one time, we found out that she had fallen in her unit. She had one of those emergency buttons on a chain around her neck she could call if she needed help. My sister eventually found out she was on the floor of her unit and couldn't get up. When she was asked, "Why didn't you press your emergency button?" she replied with something like this: "Well, I thought this was my time when Jesus was coming to take me home, so I didn't want to stop that." She had no doubt where she was going when she died.

Now in the video interview I did with her I asked her about the topic of death. Here is what she said:

[Ken] And so your father lived till, what, 92?

[Mum] My father lived to 92, and my half-sister lived till she was 91. My mother lived till she was 86. But, you know, with these problems that I have, and I can't walk very well, I ask the Lord to take me home sometimes, but He says it's not time yet.

[Ken] But you're ready to go when it's time to go?

[Mum] Absolutely.

[Ken] And so you're not worried about that.

[Mum] Well, you don't die. You know, you just go through the valley of the shadow of death. You just walk through the shadow. You don't go into it. You walk through the shadow, and you go to be with the Lord. That's what happens.

[Ken] And you're looking forward to that?

[Mum] Have you thought about that? Just go through the shadow?

There she was wanting to teach me while I was doing the video to make sure I knew about what the Bible taught.

Memorials

In a cemetery in Brisbane at a place called Mt. Gravatt, are these gravestones.

These are memorials. Their bodies were buried here to return to dust as God, in Genesis, tells us will happen: *"By the sweat of your face you shall eat bread, till you return to the ground, for out of it you were taken; for you are dust, and to dust you shall return"* (Genesis 3:19). Dad, Mum, and Robert are not in those graves, as they are with the Lord for eternity. They've all gone through the shadow of death as all

must because of our sin in Adam. One day, for those of us who have received God's gift of salvation we will meet them in heaven. What a day of rejoicing that will be.

Till we meet again.